Financing the

MW00795086

"In the closing words of *The General Theory,* John Maynard Keynes declared: 'the ideas of economists and political philosophers, both when they are right and when they are wrong, are more powerful than is commonly understood. Indeed the world is ruled by little else. Practical men, who believe themselves to be quite exempt from intellectual influences, are usually slaves of some defunct economist.'

Bob Hockett's mission in this powerful treatise is to free us from defunct, orthodox thinking about the purposes of public and private finance, the supposed incompatibility of justice and efficiency, and the putative divergence of prosperity and sustainability. All of these false tradeoffs, he shows us, are just that: false. The key is to get the finance right. An interdisciplinary tour de force."

—Paul Allen McCulley, Former Managing Director and Chief Economist, *PIMCO*; Adjunct Professor of Finance, *Georgetown McDonough School of Business*

"Critics of the Green New Deal, including many from the left, once objected that tackling both climate change and economic inequality simultaneously would make failure in both domains more likely. No longer. The unfolding COVID-19 pandemic has made clear that the far bigger risk, as Robert Hockett has argued for years, lies in failure to meet these challenges together and now.

Many also once worried that Americans would be unwilling to undertake the required WWII-scale mobilization that a Green New Deal would entail. But because a massive infusion of public investment will be required to revive our economy in any event, we now ask, why not focus that investment on our most pressing problems?—again as Robert Hockett has long asked.

Even having mustered the will to act, however, the required mobilization will be a dauntingly complex financial and logistical undertaking. In painstaking detail, Bob Hockett's masterful blueprint shows how to do it."

—Robert H. Frank, Henrietta Johnson Louis Professor of Management, *Cornell University*; Author, *Under the Influence: Putting Peer Pressure to Work*

"As the old saying has it, 'Any jackass can kick down a barn, but it takes a carpenter to build one.' After half a century of misguided demolition of the financial architecture that underpinned shared national and global prosperity, public purpose finance has found a master builder as well as a master scholar in Robert C. Hockett."

—Michael Lind, Professor, *Lyndon B. Johnson School of Public Affairs, University of Texas at Austin*; Author, *Land of Promise: An Economic History of the United States*

"State investment is often driven by a national mission to boost development or security—think of the railway boom, the creation of the interstate highway system, or the development of the internet, all of which were fueled by the public sector. In this important new book, Robert C. Hockett lays out how to do industrial policy, American-style, and tells us why a Green New Deal is crucial to the future of not only U.S. economic growth, but liberal democracy itself."

—Rana Foroohar, Global Economic Analyst, *CNN*; Global Business Columnist and Associate Editor, *Financial Times*

"You might disagree with some of these proposals, as do I. But you cannot afford to ignore them. Anyone who wants a sustainable future will have to develop means of assuring it that are as creative and ambitious—as 'out of the box'—as these."

—Robert J. Shiller, Nobel Laureate and Sterling Professor of Economics, *Yale University*

Robert C. Hockett

Financing the Green New Deal

A Plan of Action and Renewal

Robert C. Hockett
Cornell University
Ithaca, NY, USA

ISBN 978-3-030-48449-1   ISBN 978-3-030-48450-7   (eBook)
https://doi.org/10.1007/978-3-030-48450-7

This Palgrave Macmillan imprint is published by the registered company Springer Nature Switzerland AG.
The registered company address is: Gewerbestrasse 11, 6330 Cham, Switzerland

I'd like to dedicate this monograph to U.S. Congresswoman Alexandria Ocasio-Cortez and her remarkable team, whose Chief of Staff first commissioned it and whose every deed inspires it.

Foreword

"How are you going to pay for it?"

It was March 20, 2019. In a little over a week, Representative Alexandria Ocasio-Cortez would be going live to millions of people on MSNBC for an hour-long town hall-style discussion of the Green New Deal. As I worked on the brief she would use to prepare for it (a 'brief' that ended up being a little over 50 pages long), I stared at the question that had come to be a part of every bit of news and discussion about the Green New Deal:

"How are you going to pay for it?"

It had been a pretty wild journey to get here. Just a year earlier, I was the campaign manager for Alexandria's primary election campaign where the Green New Deal was only an idea. After her upset victory, I was named Alexandria's Chief of Staff and charged with fleshing out the Green New Deal. Our team scrambled to turn this idea into a blueprint to tackle climate change that listed out, sector by sector, how America could mobilize its economy to build a carbon neutral society while drastically improving the standard of living for as many people as possible. Yes, it was a big plan, but that's only because creating a carbon neutral society is a massive undertaking. But, as were asked over and over again: how were we going to pay for it?

I knew that though many asked this question as a kind of gotcha, many others did wonder about this earnestly. And there WERE some clear answers to this question. We knew that any plan to actually reverse climate change as fast as is needed would probably involve mobilizing trillions of dollars of capital to change almost every sector of our economy. But we also knew that not tackling the problem would likely cause tens or hundreds of trillions of dollars in damage in the long run, dwarfing any money spent on a solution. We knew that the lion's share of the money that we proposed spending in the Green New Deal was in the form of investment in industry to not just "greenify" but upgrade everything from agriculture to automobiles to housing—the kind of spending that costs money in the short term, but makes money in the long term by developing and growing our economy. These were fine answers for television, but we also knew that there was a deeper question within this question that would require a real plan should a Green New Deal ever come to pass. And that was the question of how, exactly, we would finance a Green New Deal to mobilize the trillions of dollars in capital effectively.

I knew this was a question someone with real expertise and knowledge would have to create a plan for. Someone with both depth and breadth of knowledge of how our economy works and both public and private financing mechanisms. But most of all, it would need to be somebody who could think of all this while having a deep empathy for people—someone who could really understand the kind of suffering such a large scale transformation could cause if done wrong, but also the kind of widespread prosperity it could create if done right. And as if by a miracle, this was right around when I got put in touch with Bob.

Now, I knew of Bob by reputation. My wife had gone to law school at Cornell and had told me about her law professor, Robert Hockett—the guy that everyone knew was an absolute genius, prolific with his work, and who was unafraid to explore the ideas others wouldn't touch. My colleagues on the Financial Services Committee in Congress told me he was a reliable advisor whose experience working at the Fed and the International Monetary Fund gave him an in-depth knowledge of how financial systems in America worked. I had heard of him from my colleague Zack Exley, who had gotten to know him over the last year, and told me about the guy who won a Rhodes scholarship and then opted to spend a year living amongst the homeless community to truly understand what they are going through.

But when I talked to Bob for the first time, the first thing I noticed was something that can't get across on paper: Bob's energy and passion is a force of nature. And while it was clear that Bob had a mastery of several subjects, easily talking about everything from the law to public finance to ancient Chinese history, he also had the unique ability to actually communicate this expertise in a way that anyone—even I!—could grasp.

Over the next several months, I got to know Bob better as I called him often to get his advice on a variety of topics. Rep. Ocasio-Cortez sits on the Financial Services Committee, so I would regularly pepper Bob with questions about everything from the payday lending industry to the 2007 financial crash and how to be resilient against a new one. And every time, Bob gave me extremely thoughtful and deep answers, often not just to the question I'd ask but the question I should be asking, and through these conversations I learned who, exactly, Bob is and what drives him. Yes, Bob is a genius, a creative polymath able to come up with solutions others can't see. And he's also an incredibly kind person, patient and understanding. But I learned that, despite a long, successful career, Bob is that rare person who does not let the trappings of success keep him from continuing to push boundaries, explore, produce, and explain because at the end of the day, Bob is driven by something much bigger than his own career: a drive to truly change this world to be a better place.

Bob had already worked with New Consensus (a think tank that had produced much of the intellectual foundation for a Green New Deal) to create a 14-page explainer on the Green New Deal, which included a short section on financing. When I learned that Bob was going to flesh this out to work on a full, detailed financing plan, I was ecstatic. And, as ever, Bob was thorough, innovative, and fast in executing the project: he started in June, and by July he had drafted the full plan—the plan that you now find in this book.

The plan you find here bears all the hallmarks both of our Green New Deal vision and of Bob's way of thinking about public and private finance. It is characteristically respectful of existing institutions and divisions of labor on the one hand, while not hesitating to adjust or repurpose those institutions and dispense with obsolete orthodoxies when necessary on the other hand. It also, like seemingly everything Bob does, starts from first principles and then builds from the ground up in explaining and justifying everything that it proposes. And, of course, it exhibits Bob's characteristic comfort with multiple disciplines and their histories.

Here you will find a plan that reforms all—but also only—what needs reform in order to fulfill the Green New Deal's ambitious agenda. It is, like the Green New Deal vision itself, as attentive to justice and inclusion as it is to efficiency and growth, seeing in these things not "trade-offs," but deeply complementary ideals. It also, again like the Green New Deal vision itself, aims to facilitate collaboration between the public and private sectors alike, as well as among local, state, and federal levels of government. In this sense it takes both our "mixed economy" and our "federalist" form of governance as givens and then works to optimize their harmonious functioning in the cause of an economic revitalization that will make literally all of us richer while also preserving our planet and making full productive participants of everyone in our society.

Throughout the design and discussion, Bob as usual carefully explains precisely why he proposes what he does, and why any less would be insufficient while any more would be unnecessary. In so doing he makes ample use not only of his theoretical and historical learning, but also of his practical experience in both public and private sector financial institutions. His proposed revamping and recombining of existing institutions accordingly bears the stamp not only of academic authority but also of rich practical experience, common sense, and incredible empathy.

So, how are we going to pay for it? The answer is in your hands.

San Francisco, CA, USA   Saikat Chakrabarti

Acknowledgments

Many brilliant and inspiring friends have offered helpful comments and suggestions in connection with this monograph's first draft, and others I owe longer-standing debts of love, gratitude, and admiration. Among those I owe special thanks are Randy Abreu; Dan Alpert; Kaushik Basu; Alex Beaton; Andrés Bernal; Mark Blyth; Ellen Brown; Jon Cardinal; Saikat Chakrabarti; Demond Drummer; Zack Exley; Rana Foroohar; Bob Frank; Ty Gellasch; Billie Gendell; Elizabeth Graber; Chris Griswold; Warren Gunnels; Aaron James; Stephanie Kelton; NY Assemblyman Ron Kim; the late Tammy Lothian; Kami Malwatte; Jerry Mashaw; Paul McCulley; Sara Nelson; Rep. Alexandria Ocasio-Cortez & Team; Saule Omarova; Caleb Orr; Eswar Prasad; Bharat Ramamurti; Dan Riffle; John Roemer; NY State Senator Julia Salazar; Sen. Bernie Sanders & Team; Sherle Schwenninger; Bob Shiller; Sophia Siegler; my colleagues with Ithaca Sunrise and NYC Sunrise, in particular Marissa Lansing, Mike Moritz, and Miles Goodrich; Alan Thomas; Corbin Trent; Roberto Mangabeira Unger; Sen. Elizabeth Warren & Team; and the late Erik Wright. It should not be thought that all named here endorse all that I argue in this book; indeed that is doubtful. I hope it will be understood, however, that I have learned from them all. Thank you, Friends.

Contents

List of Figures

Introduction

In February 2019, U.S. Representative Alexandria Ocasio-Cortez and U.S. Senator Edward Markey, joined by multiple Hose and Senate co-sponsors, introduced what has since been called the 'Green New Deal Resolution' to Congress.[1] The Resolution calls for the White House and Congress to develop and implement a comprehensive plan to mobilize the American economy for a just, efficient, and expeditious transition to a revitalized and carbon-neutral economy by 2030.

The principal reason for the Resolution's urgent timeframe—just over a decade—is by now well understood: U.S. government climate scientists and their counterparts around the world have determined that we cannot reasonably assume there is any more time than this to prevent an irreversible and catastrophic climatic tipping point's being reached, beyond which neither our own nor many other species will be likely to survive.[2]

---

[1] See 116th Congress (2019–2020), H. Res. 109, Recognizing the Duty of the Federal Government to Create a Green New Deal, available at https://www.congress.gov/bill/116th-congress/house-resolution/109/text; and 116th Congress (2019–2020), S. Res. 59, Recognizing the Duty of the Federal Government to Create a Green New Deal, available at https://www.congress.gov/bill/116th-congress/senate-resolution/59?q=%7B%22search%22%3A%5B%22green+new+deal%22%5D%7D&s=2&r=3

[2] See U.S. Global Change Research Program, Fourth National Climate Assessment (NCA4) (2018), available at https://nca2018.globalchange.gov/downloads/NCA4_Report-in-Brief.pdf

On the way to that bleak ending, moreover, extreme socio-economic injustice and associated political breakdown—now well underway in nations already hard-hit by environmental crisis, as well as in adjacent nations toward which literally millions of climate refugees are mass-migrating—can be expected to hasten as well. Environmental disaster and associated social, economic, and political dysfunction, in other words, ironically could themselves stand in the way of collectively addressing the processes driving these breakdowns themselves.

The one silver lining to this 'one underlying cause, many crises' scenario is that, just as climate change is driving our social, economic, and political breakdowns, so can comprehensively *addressing* our climate crisis *arrest and reverse* those interconnected breakdowns. The key is to plan carefully and intelligently. It is, in other words, to get the full Green New Deal right. And because the Green New Deal Resolution has drawn broad public support both at home and abroad, most of it non-partisan, the prospects for success on this score are bright—provided we act and act fast.

Of all the planning that must be done to make of the Green New Deal a rapid success, probably none is more important than, even if some are equally important to, Green New Deal *financing*. There are at least two related reasons, both of which prompt and inform the present monograph.

The first reason is that any economic mobilization effort, such as the Green New Deal effort must be, is an effort to *marshal and channel both efforts and resources*. People must *work*, work *together*, and have access to *resources* to work *with* in transforming the physical infrastructure, both social and economic, on which all people who constitute our society and economy base their activities. This includes everything from the facilities through which we produce and add value, to the networks, organizations, and other mechanisms through which we channel and distribute value inputs and outputs, on down to the homes, towns, and cityscapes in which we live, love, create, and recreate. And *financing* just *is* marshaling and channeling in those senses.

The second reason finance is crucial to effective Green New Deal planning is that any truly nationwide mobilization of the kind envisaged by the Green New Deal must be thoughtfully synchronized to avoid inefficient duplications of, and efficiency-undermining crossed-purposes among, our joint Green New Deal efforts. The effort must, in other words, be the action equivalent of a single big balance sheet's worth of resource and effort allocation. And there is no better perch from which to help harmonize separate efforts across states, regions and localities, and public and private sector institutions, in this way than our *financial system*—the system that does all that allocating.

The present monograph accordingly lays out the broad frame of a Green New Deal financial architecture. The aim is to map out a 'flow-structure' through which efforts can be synchronized, and resources both marshaled and allocated, in a manner well adapted to efficiently and expeditiously implementing the full Green New Deal—all component parts of it.

In addition to mapping out how Green New Deal finance can be made to work efficiently and expeditiously, this monograph also indicates how to structure Green New Deal finance in a manner that advances the cross-cutting goals of (a) maximum financial and economic inclusion across the entirety of our population; (b) maximally democratic decision-making, including a proper division of labor among the distinct 'levels' of national, regional, state and local self-government; and (c) an appropriate division of roles among 'public' and 'private' modes of productive activity and decision-making—that is, among units of government, private and mixed public-private enterprises, and labor organizations.

The monograph proceeds as follows. Chapter 1 concisely but comprehensively recapitulates the Green New Deal's animating vision and key project fields. Chapter 2 then derives from that vision and set of projects the principal goals that an optimal Green New Deal finance plan should aim to achieve. Chapter 3 then elaborates an institutional infrastructure well suited to achieving that aim—again, the efficient and expeditious mobilization and allocation of labor and material resources to transform and upgrade the nation's economy, in a manner consistent with goals (a) through (c) just noted. Chapter 4 then briefly considers variations on and proposed alternatives to the Plan sketched in Chap. 3, using the latter as benchmark in evaluating the former. The monograph then concludes and looks forward.

1

The Green New Deal in Brief Outline

The finance plan elaborated in this monograph must be understood in relation to what it is meant to finance—the Green New Deal. The aims, ambition, and structure of the former are outgrowths of the aims, ambitions, and structure of the latter. It will accordingly be helpful concisely but comprehensively to recapitulate the first before elaborating the second. We can best order that recapitulation, in turn, by reference to what's 'green,' what is 'new,' and what's 'dealt-with' in the Green New Deal.

1.1 'Green'

During their first weeks in the new U.S. Congress circa January and February of 2019, U.S. Representative Alexandria Ocasio-Cortez, Senator Edward Markey, and their colleagues did something no other American political figure had managed for decades. They got their whole country, and indeed much of the world, talking about massively transformative public investment as a real prospect.[1]

---

[1] See again 116th Congress (2019–2020), supra note 1.

© The Author(s) 2020
R. C. Hockett, *Financing the Green New Deal*,
https://doi.org/10.1007/978-3-030-48450-7_1

The Green New Deal exceeds in scale and scope all major undertakings of U.S. federal, state, and local governments since both its namesake—Franklin Roosevelt's original New Deal—and the mobilization effort for the Second World War in 1940s, respectively.[2] And this is true irrespective of what measure of 'size' one might use—geographic and cross-sectoral scope, number of firms and sub-federal units of government that will be playing a role, segments of the population who will be playing a role, dollar value of real expenditures, dollar value of expenditures as a percentage of GDP, and so on.[3]

Ambition on such a scale has, at least since the time of President Eisenhower's ambitious interstate highway system and President Kennedy's space program, tended to draw fear and naysaying from the timid, the cynical, and the financially uninformed. The Green New Deal has been no exception. Predictable expressions of skepticism and incredulity, along with familiar 'what about partisan gridlock' and 'how will we pay for it?' queries, have abounded since early 2019. Even some self-styled *progressive* politicians have hedged their bets, approving 'the concept' while studiously shying away from declaring on any particular instantiation.[4]

Against such a backdrop, one does well to recognize that 'size matters' where the Green New Deal is concerned—and matters in ways that the politically demoralized, the fiscally austere, and tepid allies alike tend to miss. The problems the Green New Deal addresses, in short, are problems where bigger is better, is imperative, and is, paradoxically, more politically feasible and 'affordable' too where responding to crisis is concerned.

To begin with the imperative part: The overwhelming weight of climate science prediction avers that average global temperatures have now crossed a threshold, and are still climbing at a rate, that leaves no option

---

[2] Historians often now merge these consecutive periods together under the rubric of what's called 'The *Long* New Deal.' See, for example, Hockett & Gunn-Wright, *The Green New Deal: Mobilizing for a Just, Prosperous, and Sustainable Economy*, New Consensus White Paper (2019), available at https://papers.ssrn.com/sol3/papers.cfm?abstract_id=3342494

[3] Id. See also Robert Hockett, 'Pay for the Green New Deal Now or Spend More Later,' Financial Times, 3 February 2019, available at https://www.ft.com/content/046e7c30-23c8-11e9-b20d-5376ca5216eb

[4] See sources cited id.

now but to reverse course on carbon emissions post haste.[5] The consequence of inaction will be the extinction of both the human and other species of life, while the consequences of further foot-dragging will be astronomically high costs brought on by continuing and ever more frequent environmental calamities.[6] It will 'cost more' to do nothing or not enough, in other words, than it will to do what needs doing. Where climate change is concerned, the question we face now is accordingly not whether or even when, but is *how*—and how *quickly*—to address them.

Enter the Green New Deal. What separates its advocates from generic progressives and even earlier generations of climate advocates is its recognition that climate change must now be reversed urgently, quickly, and comprehensively. The Green New Deal's advocates also recognize more— namely, that 'going big' here is actually to go more politically and fiscally feasibly too. That is part of what makes the Green New Deal 'new' and a 'deal,' the next two subjects to be taken up below. But it also results in the Green New Deal's being far more comprehensively 'green' than that word alone might initially suggest.

As advocates envision it, the Green New Deal will comprise a full portfolio of mutually complementary and critically necessary mitigation and renewal projects, now known as the Green New Deal *Project Fields*.[7] All of these, advocates aver, will contribute to the restoration of both a healthy planet and a just, prosperous, and sustainable economy that treats (a) all Americans as valued members of society and (b) the environment as their home. These Project Fields include, among others:

• Building 'smart,' energy-efficient national power grids to enable transition to renewable power, including energy storage modalities and technologies as well as improvements that complement other Green New Deal projects;

---

[5] See again U.S. Global Change Research Program, Fourth National Climate Assessment (NCA4) (2018), supra note 2.
[6] Id.
[7] See sources cited supra, note 5.

- Overhauling American transportation systems to eliminate green-house gas emissions and capture as much energy efficiency as is physically possible;
- Replacing fossil fuel power generation with wind, solar, hydro, and other renewables. Also expanding existing renewable power sources and deploying new production and storage capacity to meet 100% of national power demand through renewable sources;
- Upgrading every residential and industrial building for state-of-the-art energy efficiency, comfort, and safety. This will open millions of new high-wage jobs in every community and will be designed to foster ownership by communities, with the work being done by local firms, organizations, and co-ops. It will also make startup capital available to people who want to form new firms and co-ops, and take care to invest especially in communities that have been denied capital and development for generations;
- Investing in and working with U.S. industry to eliminate greenhouse gas emissions from production and to capture as much energy efficiency as is physically possible. This will involve massive investments to industrial firms to undertake energy efficiency upgrades and do the work of transitioning away from fossil fuels;
- Investing in and working with American farmers to reduce greenhouse gas emissions from agriculture and capture as much energy efficiency as is physically possible, and to encourage transition to more sustainable, locally focused agriculture. Also working to improve the health of farmers and farm workers and the quality of area food supplies;
- Making adequate capital, technical expertise, and other forms of assistance available to all communities, organizations, and business firms in the nation; also investing in technological R&D to support all Green New Deal projects—for example, in battery technologies, energy efficient materials, etc.;
- Upgrading water infrastructure to ensure universal access to clean water in every community; also carrying out coastal remediation projects and other overdue ecosystem projects to protect and heal endangered and fragile ecosystems; and
- Making green technology, industry, expertise, products, and services a principal export of the U.S., with the aim of becoming the undisputed

international leader in helping other countries transition to greenhouse gas neutral economies and bringing about a *global* Green New Deal. Also promoting global cooperation and exchange of green technology, industry, expertise, products, and services and encouraging a global Green New Deal.

The 'green' character of these projects is presumably obvious. It should also be clear, however, that together the projects involve nothing less than a comprehensive overhaul and revitalization of the nation's entire infrastructural and industrial base. And this is part of what makes the Green New Deal, at least in comparison to all other national projects undertaken over the past 80 years, 'new.'

1.2 'New'

In virtue of both its fiscal and its political scale and scope, the Green New Deal truly is 'new' in comparison to previous environmental and economic initiatives commenced since the end of the Second World War. Advocates view this not as an unfortunate yet necessary blemish, but as an affirmative *advantage*. We can begin with the fiscal factor here, then turn to the political in the next subsection, on the Green New Deal's status as a 'deal.'

The suggestion that size is a virtue where the Green New Deal's fiscal features are concerned might ring counterintuitive at first. But a moment's thought quickly reveals its basis. There are at least three reasons, the first two of which will be quickly accessible even to untutored non-expert intuition.[8]

The first reason stems from the 'scale economies' familiar even to orthodox economists—not to mention most businesses. Any productive activity—including that of climate mitigation—occasions both fixed costs and variable costs. Because even small-scale activity brings fixed costs, fixed costs per unit of activity tend to diminish as the scale of activity rises. This in turn means that *average* costs per unit decline—at least

---

[8] Id.

to the point at which 'diminishing returns' kick-in in many industries. And where climate mitigation is concerned, the scale of the threat that humanity now faces is so enormous that returns are not apt to diminish for many years, if not decades, to come.

The second reason that a bigger Green New Deal will likely be fiscally more feasible—'more affordable'—than a small-bore initiative stems from the 'snowball effect' that one typically sees in connection with most forms of environmental and infrastructural degradation. Anyone who has noticed how much more quickly an already shrunken bar of soap washes away than does a comparable mass from a fresh bar of soap, or how one sporting injury one suffers can lead on quite quickly to additional, cascading injuries as she changes how she walks to accommodate it, will have an inkling already of this recursively self-exponentiating dynamic.

Environmental and infrastructural degradation are like this. Their paces accelerate as early harms damage capacities to compensate for later harms. Hence the 'cost acceleration' phenomenon to which economists often refer, and the 'feedback effects' climate scientists cite as our presently most daunting perils. Most people likely understand this, but fewer seem apt to draw its upshot absent its being pointed explicitly out: namely, that acting faster yields more 'bang for the buck' than does acting sluggishly.

Acting faster here means spending more now rather than later—it means 'front-loading' our efforts. Likewise the targeting first of economically disadvantaged communities—inner cities, rural outposts, etc.—for Green New Deal projects: restoring the local environment and economy of a Flint, Michigan, or New Orleans, Louisiana, will tend to yield more immediate 'payoff' than will that of, say, Palo Alto in California or Chappaqua in New York. And this, as it happens, is one reason that Green New Dealers are quick to aver that the *justice* and *environmental* ambitions of the Green New Deal are *not practically independent* of or orthogonal to one another, but are in effect *joined at the hip*—mutually reinforcing and of a piece with each other, programmatically speaking.

The third fiscal reason that advocates aim to 'go big' on the Green New Deal is best considered in relation to the ubiquitous but misguided 'how will we pay' question noted above.[9] One should first note that 'how do we pay' actually is code for something else. Republics that issue their own monetary claims upon resources and tax their own 'lenders' don't have to 'raise' money; they 'create' money by issuing and spending. This means the 'how do we pay' question actually proxies for a distinct, 'what about inflation' question—the only *real* constraint upon spending by democracies.[10] But once we see this, Green New Deal advocates note further, we see another reason to 'swing for the fences' as Green New Dealers urge— namely, so that Green New Deal projects increase *production and productive capacity* as quickly as they grow the *money supply*.[11]

The key here is that inflation—like deflation—is always a *relation*. It is a matter of money quantity or velocity in relation to goods and services quantity. Too much money in relation to a given stock of goods and services is inflationary; too little, as has been painfully relearned from 2008 to this day, is deflationary.[12]

But this is another reason, Green New Dealers note, that 'going big' with the Green New Deal is far less likely to budge inflation numbers from their still stubbornly low sub-2% rates than would 'going small.' For the Green New Deal plan is to *ramp-up* production, installation, and ultimately even exportation of all manner of new, carbon-free products, services, and infrastructure—from solar panels, windmills, and batteries, through new plants and charging stations, to 'smart' power grids and beyond.[13]

The Green New Deal is not going to require 'new taxes' or 'unsustainable debt' while inflation is nonexistent—that is to say, while production is keeping pace with the money that finances it. Only an uptick in

---

[9] See Robert Hockett, *The Green New Deal: How We Will Pay for It Isn't 'A Thing' – and Inflation Isn't Either*, FORBES, January 16, 2019, available at https://www.forbes.com/sites/rhockett/2019/01/16/the-green-new-deal-how-we-will-pay-for-it-isnt-a-thing-and-inflation-isnt-either/. For further legal and theoretical background, see Robert Hockett, *A Fixer-Upper for Finance*, 87 WASHINGTON UNIVERSITY LAW REVIEW 1213 (2009) (introducing 'credit-money modulation' as principal task of financial regulation); and Robert Hockett, *The Macroprudential Turn: From Institutional 'Safety and Soundness' to Systemic 'Financial Stability' in Financial Supervision*, 9 VIRGINIA LAW & BUSINESS REVIEW 1 (2015) (developing 'macroprudential toolkit' for the finance-regulatory task of modulating credit-money aggregates).

[10] Id.

[11] Id.

[12] Id.

[13] Id.

inflation would require any 'stepping on the brakes.' And since (a) well over $7 trillion in tax cut and war expenditures in recent years have *not* triggered inflation in the U.S. or elsewhere, (b) the Fed has yet to get inflation consistently *up* to its 2% *target* over the past decade plus from *below*, and (c) the Green New Deal will, as just noted, produce new *goods and services* to keep pace with and absorb its *expenditures*, there is no more reason to let abstract fears halt progress here than there was to let it halt our recent past wars or tax cuts; indeed there is less, as those earlier cases of expenditure were not productive.[14]

As Green New Dealers see it, then, not since the U.S.'s move to a wartime economy in late 1941 has the U.S. enjoyed as much 'fiscal space' for productive enhancement as it does now.[15] And the nation *must fill* that space now thanks to 'exogenous' developments that are every bit as 'existentially' perilous as was the peril that Pearl Harbor heralded in that earlier era. The looming climate catastrophe, as well as the nation's catastrophic and still-worsening poverty, pandemic, opioid, and inequality crises, confronts the U.S. and the wider world with what the great American philosopher William James once called 'the *moral equivalent* of war.' And when a republic is waging a war, especially a war for its very survival, it does not 'low-ball' or 'pinch pennies.' That would be suicide. And it would be 'false economy.'

1.3 'Deal'

The scale and scope of the Green New Deal are a breakthrough not only in relation to fiscal space, but also in relation to political space. Green New Dealers see the initiative as the single greatest exercise in deliberative and participatory democracy that the U.S. has yet undertaken.[16] It is an

[14] Id.

[15] Id.

[16] See, for example, Robert Hockett, *Who Will Make the Green New Deal? Literally All of Us*, FORBES, February 12, 2019, available at https://www.forbes.com/sites/rhockett/2019/02/12/who-will-make-the-green-new-deal-literally-all-of-us/. See generally MICHAEL HILTZIK, THE NEW DEAL: A MODERN HISTORY (2011); DAVID M. KENNEDY, FREEDOM FROM FEAR: THE AMERICAN PEOPLE IN DEPRESSION AND WAR, 1929–1945 (2001); WILLIAM LEUCHTENBURG, FRANKLIN ROOSEVELT AND THE NEW DEAL: 1932–1940 (1963); and ARTHUR M. SCHLESINGER, JR., THE COMING OF THE NEW DEAL, 1933–1935 (1958).

invitation to all who are here to 'deal' together with the nation's now increasingly backward economy, unraveling social and political fabric, and dying environment.[17] The best way to elaborate this point is to begin with the Green New Deal Resolution introduced in Congress the first week of February 2019—a document to which over 70 U.S. Representatives, multiple Senators, and nearly all Democratic presidential candidates of that year ultimately signed on.[18]

Accompanying all the excitement around the Green New Deal Resolution were queries concerning the status of the document in the fuller Green New Deal process, along with discussions about what the brief document's broad statements of principle, hope, and aspiration would entail. The definitive Green New Dealer reply to the latter discussions was and is easy: *It is up to us all.*[19] And that is because of the answer to the first query, which was and is that the Green New Deal Resolution is simply the opening gavel of an extended national deliberation—a deliberation that includes literally all in America, not to mention the world, and effectively began with announcement of the Green New Deal Resolution itself.[20]

Two facts about the original New Deal, from which the Green New Deal takes part of its name, bear remembering in this connection. The first is that the New Deal was never a '*done* deal,' much less a deal that was done by day one. Rather than a single enactment passed into law early on in a single presidential administration, the New Deal was an organic process—an ongoing project of national recovery and renewal.[21] It unfolded over the course of a decade, and took shape in the form of literally scores of statutes passed by Congress and signed into law by President Roosevelt after careful study, long public hearings, and final decision.[22]

The second fact of the New Deal that is helpful to remember in the present connection is that it had projects in every precinct of the

---

[17] Id.
[18] See again 116th Congress (2019–2020), supra note 1.
[19] See again Hockett, *Who Will Make the Green New Deal? Literally All of Us*, supra note 37.
[20] Id.
[21] See again sources cited supra, note 37.
[22] Id.

country.[23] All Americans were to benefit, irrespective of political affiliation, vocation, or geographic location. This wasn't only smart politics of the 'give them all a piece of this' variety. It was democracy. It was justice. It was about using the populace's commonly owned and operated instrumentality—our federal government—for the benefit of literally all of us.[24]

This is not to say that the New Deal at all times worked equally well for all Americans. It is widely understood that there were flaws in the implementation, for example, owing in part to the spirit of experimentation and 'trial and error' strategy deliberately adopted by the New Dealers,[25] and in part to the casual racism or sexism of various officials and business firms in the more overtly racist and sexist U.S. of the 1930s and 1940s.[26] But the point is that the New Deal was meant to be truly national in scope, even while also local and sectional in execution.

All of this bears significant implications for the *Green* New Deal. It means first that the Green New Deal too will develop organically over the course of a decade—a decade in which literally all Americans will be proposing, critiquing, and counter-proposing, all in a spirit of joint deliberation about how best to rescue our planet and rejuvenate our economy and society in the process.[27] And it means second that Green New Dealers intend, without cavil or qualification, and without shame or embarrassment, for the Green New Deal to benefit *literally all Americans.*[28] And since the present era is happily less starkly racist and sexist than were earlier times, 'all' here means all genders and ethnicities far more literally than it did in the 1930s and 1940s.

When she began her orientation as NY-14's new Representative in the new House of Representatives early in 2019, Representative Ocasio-Cortez delighted her constituents and many more Americans by posting

---

[23] Id.

[24] Id.

[25] Id.

[26] Id. See also, for example, IRA KATZNELSON, FEAR ITSELF: THE NEW DEAL AND THE ORIGINS OF OUR TIME (2014); also IRA KATZNELSON, WHEN AFFIRMATIVE ACTION WAS WHITE: AN UNTOLD HISTORY OF RACIAL INEQUALITY IN TWENTIETH CENTURY AMERICA (2006). The *Green* New Deal aims both to steer clear of that injustice and to rectify the legacies of that injustice with which we still live.

[27] See again sources cited supra, note 37.

[28] Id.

phone video footage of each day's events on social media platforms.[29] What charmed so many about this was how it included all her constituents in the experience of assuming her responsibilities as their Representative. They were there with her, in effect, just as assuredly as they had put her there.

This was participation in government—this was democracy—of a kind that the U.S. has not seen since the last great user of new media to share with his constituents, Franklin Roosevelt, entered 'America's living rooms' regularly in his 'fireside chats' of the 1930s. This is precisely how those working on the Green New Deal want *it* to proceed. All want it to develop organically over a decade just as the first New Deal did.[30] They want it to do so with the benefit of literally all Americans' wisdom and ideas.[31] And they want it to work *for* the benefit of literally all of them too.[32]

Only this way do 'the People' get the Green New Deal right. Only this way will it be both suitably green and properly democratic. And only this way will it be a 'deal' that is authentically 'new.' But all of this requires financing in the sense elaborated above. It requires a finance *plan* of a scale, scope, and structure commensurate with the scale, scope, and structure of the Green New Deal itself. And so to that this monograph now turns.

---

[29] See, for example, https://www.youtube.com/watch?v=4fwtn_L2qVo
[30] See again sources cited supra, note 37.
[31] Id.
[32] Id.

2

What a Green New Deal Finance Plan Should Do

Turning now from the Green New Deal itself to its financing, it will be well to start with a reminder of what any finance plan, not just a Green New Deal Finance Plan, is *for*. That is to say, what financing is meant to *do*. While the Green New Deal is unique among recent national projects in many ways as just elaborated, its need of financing is not. All that will set Green New Deal financing apart from other cases of project financing is what is unique to the Green New Deal itself—its size, scope, and duration.

2.1 Mobilize and Allocate Resources

In the first instance, to finance any project is to muster the people and resources that are needed to carry out the project. In a commercial society and market exchange economy such as ours, that means to secure the funding necessary to pay the people and purchase the resources that combine to execute the project.

In the second instance, to finance an exceptionally *ambitious* and *complex* project like the Green New Deal is to *organize* the *deployment* of

© The Author(s) 2020
R. C. Hockett, *Financing the Green New Deal*,
https://doi.org/10.1007/978-3-030-48450-7_2

people and resources involved in the project in a *coherent manner*, one that is well adapted to efficient execution of the project. This is again because in an exchange economy such as our own one organizes work-flows and resource flows by organizing money flows.

'Mustering' and 'organizing' in this context are accordingly matters of mobilizing and allocating.[1]

2.1.1 Mobilize

To mobilize people and resources in pursuit of a project is to bring them coherently together in effecting that project. In the U.S. right now, there are people in abundance who can work, and resources in abundance that can be deployed, in pursuit of any great national project. As a people, we're good at this. That was true of earlier national projects like the original New Deal and then Second World War efforts of the 1930s and 1940s. It will likewise be true of the Green New Deal effort of the coming decade.

The key to success is to enable our people and resources to *come together systematically* to *execute* the project. And again, in a market exchange economy such as ours, that means bringing together the *funds* with which people are paid and resources are purchased.

'Bringing funds together' in this context can be done in either or both of two ways. The first is to attract the flow of moneys already in existence toward the project in question. The second, which is available primarily to our federal, not to our state or local governments, is to issue new credit insofar as this can be done without triggering significant inflationary pressure, more on which below.

---

[1] The U.S. seems to have pioneered the understanding of finance as a tool for the mobilization and strategic allocation of abundant but under-utilized and misallocated resources. This understanding was the key to the paired public finance and national development innovations of our first Treasury Secretary, Alexander Hamilton. The model was subsequently adopted, and specifically credited to Hamilton, by Germany, Japan, and the Asian 'tiger' economies over the course of the nineteenth and twentieth centuries. See in particular FORREST MCDONALD, ALEXANDER HAMILTON (1979). See also RON CHERNOW, ALEXANDER HAMILTON (2004); BROADUS MITCHELL, ALEXANDER HAMILTON (1962); and Robert Hockett, *Pre-Liberal Autonomy and Post-Liberal Finance*, 77 LAW & CONTEMPORARY PROBLEMS 105 (2015), available at https://papers.ssrn.com/sol3/papers.cfm?abstract_id=2554100. Sources on non-U.S. jurisdictions are cited infra, Chap. 3.

The plan elaborated in this monograph capitalizes on both of these modalities—use of existing funds and generation of new funds—in mobilizing people and resources. Owing to the *complexity* of the Green New Deal across *multiple dimensions*, however, it does not stop there. It also discharges the other main function of finance—the *allocation* of efforts and resources in pursuit of the project, hence of the funds needed to fuel those efforts and secure those resources.

2.1.2   Allocate

In addition to *mobilizing* people and resources—that is, bringing them systematically together to work in unison to execute the project—a finance plan must also *allocate* funds coherently in a manner that enables the deployment of people and resources in *multiple directions*—directions that correspond to the Green New Deal's 14 Project Fields. That is, it must both distribute funds and direct those funds' use in a manner that heads-off their being used in ways that are redundant, at crossed-purposes, or otherwise counterproductive. This task is particularly critical in the case of the Green New Deal. For, as noted above, the Green New Deal is not only comprehensive and complex, but is so across at least three dimensions:

2.1.2.1   Across the Green New Deal Project Fields

The first dimension of Green New Deal complexity is that of its Project Fields. The Green New Deal Resolution names 14 such fields, all of which are of critical importance if the climate crisis is to be reversed and the planet preserved.[2] Green New Deal financing must accordingly allocate funds in a manner that adequately resources our efforts in all 14 of those 'spaces.' And it must do so in a manner that ensures that no efforts in one space unduly repeat or impede counterpart efforts in other spaces.

---

[2] See House and Senate Resolutions, supra, note 1

2.1.2.2   Across Regions, States, Localities

The Green New Deal is comprehensive and complex not only in respect of its Project Fields, but also in respect of its geographic and jurisdictional scope. With respect to geography, one of the great strengths of the original New Deal was its organizing and funding of projects in literally every Congressional district of the country.[3] This ensured that the New Deal both (a) was more just and democratic than it might otherwise have been,[4] and (b) retained broad political support and consensus. Literally everyone was meant to 'win.'[5]

With respect to jurisdiction, the U.S. is of course a federated republic, meaning that public governance occurs not only at the national—federal—level but also at intermediate state and local levels. The purpose of federated governance structures such as ours is to enhance democracy itself, by ensuring that public officials who act at the behest of the populace are as 'close,' responsive, and accountable to the people in whose name they act as possible in connection with the projects that they pursue for them.

Some public projects—for example, the Apollo mission that ultimately landed American astronauts on the moon half a century ago—are fully national in scope. Others—for example, the Tennessee Valley Authority or the Grand Cooley Dam—are more regional or local in sweep. The idea of federalism—or 'subsidiarity,' as it is called in other jurisdictions—is that *which* public officials do *what* in connection with any public project will be determined by (a) the portion of the population primarily affected by the project, and (b) the relative strengths and competencies of the 'levels' of government involved in the project.

In the case of the New Deal's Tennessee Valley Authority (TVA), for example, state and local governments had greater knowledge of the needs of, and were more directly democratically accountable to, the rural

---

[3] See again sources cited supra, note 18.
[4] See sources cited id. It must also be noted that women and racial and ethnic minorities were often excluded or denied the full measure of benefits enjoyed by white men—an injustice of American political, social, and economic arrangements of the time rather than of the New Deal as such. See again sources cited supra, note 28.
[5] With the caveat just registered.

populations to whom the TVA was meant to bring electric power. These units of government accordingly had great say in the implementary details of the TVA's rural electrification project.[6]

The federal government, by contrast, had less expertise as to local conditions, but far more access to financial and engineering resources than did any state or local government. The TVA was in consequence largely governed and operated at subnational levels of government, while being resourced primarily by an organ of the federal government—namely the Reconstruction Finance Corporation (RFC), known as 'the bank of the New Deal.'[7] There will be more to say on the RFC below.

2.1.2.3 Across Public and Private Sectors

In addition to covering distinct Project Fields and multiple levels of government, the Green New Deal, again like its predecessor the original New Deal, will straddle both the 'public' and 'private' sectors of our society. This is hardly surprising, and there are multiple reasons for saying so.

First, ours is a 'mixed' economy in which public and private have *always* worked in tandem to optimize productive activity in manners that (a) employ resources efficiently and (b) justly distribute productive opportunity and the rewards that accrue to such activity. This has been true ever since Treasury Secretary Alexander Hamilton set the nation on its economic development course during the first decade of its existence. The Green New Deal does not aim to change this longstanding background condition—indeed, it aims to restore it.[8]

Second and relatedly, the Green New Deal's guiding ambition is to make it possible for continuing productive activity in the private sector to

---

[6] See sources cited supra, note 37. Also sources cited infra, Chap. 3, in connection with the RFC.

[7] More on the RFC below.

[8] Ironically, the U.S. seems to be the only advanced country that does *not* pervasively pair private and public sectors in pursuit of national development any longer, notwithstanding the fact that this method has been known as 'the American System' ever since Hamilton invented it. See, for example, Hockett, *Pre-Liberal Autonomy and Post-Liberal Finance*, supra note 35; also Gunn-Wright & Hockett, *The Green New Deal: Mobilizing for a Just, Prosperous, and Sustainable Economy*, New Consensus White Paper (2019), available at https://papers.ssrn.com/sol3/papers.cfm?abstract_id=3342494

be conducted in manners that (a) preserve our planet and species, (b) more justly distribute the proceeds of productive activity, and (c) help to redress many injustices that are the product of having conducted productive activity in *unjust* and *suboptimal* ways in the *past*. Since all three of these goals amount in essence to constructing a new infrastructural and manufacturing platform on which still-privately conducted enterprise can be conducted, it is essential that both public and private work in tandem in that construction.

Finally third, because a non-trivial amount of Green New Deal expenditure will be public expenditure, there is an ever-present possibility, however remote at present, that inflationary pressures will at some point be generated.[9] At least that will be so until the expenditure begins to yield productivity dividends—that is, more goods and services to absorb newly issued money and credit.[10]

The simplest way to head-off this long- or medium-term risk is by ensuring that already ongoing private expenditures are partly and productively rechanneled toward the Green New Deal project itself. That way less in the way of new credit will have to be extended. What this means for present purposes is that the public sector will have to work in tandem with the private sector when it comes to attracting financial flows, at least during the early stages of implementation. This takes us to the second principal goal of any Green New Deal Finance Plan—namely, that it attracts or offsets ongoing financial flows in ways that avoid over- or under-issuance of credit.

---

[9] For a comprehensive overview of when and how to avert the danger of inflation—which at present is very remote—see Robert Hockett, *The Green New Deal: How We Will Pay for It Isn't 'A Thing'—and Inflation Isn't Either*, FORBES, January 16, 2019, available at https://www.forbes.com/sites/rhockett/2019/01/16/the-green-new-deal-how-we-will-pay-for-it-isnt-a-thing-and-inflation-isnt-either/. For further legal and theoretical background, see Robert Hockett, *A Fixer-Upper for Finance*, 87 WASHINGTON UNIVERSITY LAW REVIEW 1213 (2009) (introducing 'credit-money modulation' as principal task of financial regulation); and Robert Hockett, *The Macroprudential Turn: From Institutional 'Safety and Soundness' to Systemic 'Financial Stability' in Financial Supervision*, 9 VIRGINIA LAW & BUSINESS REVIEW 1 (2015) (developing 'macroprudential toolkit' for the finance-regulatory task of modulating credit-money aggregates).

[10] Id.

2.2   Modulate Credit Aggregates: a.k.a. Avert Inflation and Deflation

The Green New Deal will be, in comparison to other national projects of recent years, substantial. It will involve financial flows quantified not merely in millions or even billions of dollars, but in trillions of dollars. In recent historic terms, only the original New Deal and Second World War mobilizations were of comparable scale and scope.

This should not be surprising. The American Society of Civil Engineers has been warning for many years that even to repair the infrastructure we already have would require a multi-trillion-dollar investment.[11] And the Green New Deal is about more than mere infrastructure 'repair'—it is about, among other things, infrastructural modernization and optimization. The magnitude of necessary Green New Deal expenditure also is unsurprising in comparison to that of other federal expenditures in recent years. Between war expenditures and upper bracket tax cuts over the past decade and a half, upward of $10 trillion has been spent—all, it bears noting, without thus far generating inflation.[12]

Although inflationary pressures are thus far non-existent and show no signs of building, there are conceivable scenarios under which expenditures of the magnitude necessitated by the Green New Deal could eventually generate them. There are other scenarios under which they cannot. A key aim of any Green New Deal Finance Plan is accordingly that it works to ensure the realization of the latter rather than the former scenarios.

During the early period of the original New Deal, for example, productive capacity had come to be so dramatically underutilized that even massive public expenditures proved insufficient to generate even *desired* inflation; the challenge, rather, was growth-reversing *deflation*.[13] During

---

[11] See, for example, American Society of Civil Engineers, *2017 Infrastructure Report Card*, available at https://www.infrastructurereportcard.org/the-impact/economic-impact/ (2018) (Grade of 'D+,' 10-year funding gap of $2 trillion).

[12] See again Hockett, *Not a Thing*, supra note 43.

[13] See, for example, IRVING FISHER, BOOMS AND DEPRESSIONS (1932); J.M. KEYNES, A TREATISE ON MONEY (1931); and J.M. KEYNES, THE GENERAL THEORY OF EMPLOYMENT, INTEREST, AND MONEY (1936). Also Robert Hockett & Richard Vague, *Debt, Deflation, and Debacle: Of Private Debt*

the Second World War, on the other hand, in which the U.S. became involved only after post-Depression economic recovery had finally commenced, inflationary pressure did loom as a danger, and governments like those of the U.S. and the U.K. accordingly acted 'proactively' to preempt it—much as the U.S. had done during the First World War by selling 'Liberty Bonds.'[14]

The key point to remember about both inflation and deflation is that each is a *relation*—a relation between money supply and velocity on the one hand, and goods, services, and desired transaction volume on the other hand.[15] 'Too much' of the former in relation to the latter tends to generate inflationary pressure. Too little of the former in relation to the latter yields deflationary pressure. In this simple truth lies the key to financing public projects in ways that steer clear of the twin dangers of inflation and deflation. Some of these ways should be briefly elaborated in turn:

2.2.1 Targeted Allocation

The first method of inflation-avoidance is careful targeting, where possible, of expenditures toward economic sectors or geographic locales that have been chronically cash-poor or credit-poor in recent times. A previously under-resourced sector of the economy, for example, is apt to be one in which new expenditure actually brings new productive capacity and new production, thereby generating sufficient new goods and services to absorb the money that's spent and thus avoiding inflationary pressure.

Similarly, directing expenditure toward locations whose populations have been chronically under-served and under-resourced also is apt to attract private provision of goods and services to the newly served and

---

Write-Down and Public Recovery, White Paper, Federal Reserve Bank of Philadelphia (April, 2013), available at https://www.interdependence.org/wp-content/uploads/2013/04/Debt-Deflation-and-Debacle-RV-and-RH1.pdf

[14] See, for example, J.M. KEYNES, HOW TO PAY FOR THE WAR (1940).

[15] For more detail, see again Hockett, sources cited supra note 43.

resourced locales, thereby raising money-absorptive capacity in tandem with expenditure. This too, then, can be inflation-offsetting.

Because the Green New Deal's chief guiding ambition is to resource, at long last, sectors of our national economy and communities within our population that have historically been under-resourced and under-served, there is a sense in which Green New Deal expenditures will conform to the counter-inflationary stratagem just described almost 'automatically' or 'by definition.' There is accordingly very good reason from the get-go to harbor optimism about the Green New Deal's inflationary impacts.

Of course, there can be lag times between new influxes of finance and consequent growth in productive and absorptive capacity within the sectors and locales that receive those new influxes. Inflationary pressures can, at least in theory, build up during those intervals. But this simply means other stratagems should be employed to complement this one. A helpful way to order discussion of them is by proceeding from those that are more 'carrot'-like to those that are more 'stick'-like.

2.2.2 Targeted Bond Sales

There are time-honored means of blunting, buffering, or even fully offsetting inflationary impacts on those rare occasions when such pressures emerge. All Green New Deal financing mechanisms should be developed with full awareness of these methods—not because they definitively *will* prove to be needed, but because they theoretically *could* come to be needed. Familiarity with them will accordingly aid both in preempting inflationary pressures should they loom, and in preempting unwarranted *fears* of inflation when such pressures *don't* but are falsely *claimed* to loom.

One venerable inflation-preempting method is for the spending authority to 'borrow' in the same space in which it is spending, so as temporarily to *soak up* funds in quantities that offset newly *spent* funds.[16] If, for example, federal spending on or in a bustling metropolitan precinct were to add to that precinct's money supply so quickly as to generate local inflationary pressure, an obvious remedy is to 'absorb' the excess

---

[16] See again Hockett, sources cited supra note 43.

by selling bond or other investment instruments. This was, as noted above, the idea behind 'Liberty Bond' sales in 1917 and 1918 during the First World War effort.[17]

Such sales in essence temporarily swap non-spendable assets—the bonds or other financial instruments in question—for spendable ones—money. This effectively slows money supply growth in a manner preventing its outpacing goods and services supply growth, thereby averting inflationary pressure during lag times like those noted above in Sect. 2.2.1. This is, in essence, the purpose of most federal bond issuances. Indeed the U.S. Federal Reserve is quite explicit about this, conducting open market operations in U.S. Treasury securities from the New York Fed trading desk each day specifically in order to affect monetary aggregates and, with them, inter-linked interest and inflation rates.

2.2.3 Targeted Finance Regulation

Another well-established means of modulating credit-money aggregates focuses on the credit component of the money supply. This stratagem controls credit growth by regulating leverage—that is, by limiting the margin by which borrowed funds can exceed already possessed funds used in whatever transaction type is of regulatory interest.[18] In the realm of mortgage finance, for example, we prescribe minimum down payments that have to be made on any purchased home before credit may be extended to cover the remainder. This is, in essence, what a maximum permissible loan-to-value (LTV) ratio is in connection with a debt-financed home purchase; a maximum LTV of 90% is a minimum down payment requirement of 10%.[19]

Leverage regulation of this sort is pervasive in our system of financial regulation. Capital regulation of commercial banks, for example, prescribes minimal shareholder equity ratios in relation to asset portfolio

---

[17] See, for example, Robert Hockett & Daniel Alpert, 'The Budget Is Its Own "Debt Ceiling,"' *Reuters*, October 10, 2013, available at http://blogs.reuters.com/great-debate/2013/10/10/the-budget-is-its-own-debt-ceiling/

[18] See again Hockett, *Not a Thing*, supra note 43.

[19] See, for example, Robert Hockett, *Macroprudential Turn*, supra note 43.

sizes, equity in this case functioning as the bank analogue to home-buyer down-payments.[20] The so-called Net Capital Rule to which broker-dealers are subject is of the same form and purpose.[21] The key point is that credit is limited to a defined multiple of already accumulated and hence finite wealth, with the 'multiplier'—that is, the reciprocal of the mandatory leverage ratio—adjustable either to slow or to accelerate credit growth according as prices fall subject to inflationary or deflationary pressures.[22]

Although experts on financial regulation have historically been under-appreciative of the fact, this is in essence what much of financial regulation in a complex monetary economy is *for*—it is largely about what might be called 'regulation as modulation.'[23] All Green New Deal financing mechanisms should be developed with full awareness of this tool. If particular Green New Deal projects come eventually to generate inflationary pressures in particular sectors of the economy or regions of the country, for example, leverage regulation can be targeted just as bond sales or 'borrowing' can as described just above in Sect. 2.2.2.

Owing to its 'carrot' rather than 'stick'-like nature, the bond sale strategy is probably preferable as first resort in the event of inflationary pressure. Leverage regulation can then serve as first 'fallback' option, inasmuch as it does not 'confiscate' anything but simply imposes conditions on otherwise permitted lending activity. This takes us to the next stratagem, which is more confiscatory but also quite potent when necessary.

2.2.4 Targeted Taxing

A third mode of inflation preemption or elimination is to tax money when it is generated and spent in excess of goods and services provision. The mode of operation here is as simple as can be. If there is 'too much

---

[20] See 12 CFR §§ 303 & cet., available at https://www.fdic.gov/regulations/laws/federal/2013/2013-09-10_final-rule-interim.pdf

[21] See SEC Rule 15c3-1, available at https://www.sec.gov/about/offices/oia/oia_market/key_rules.pdf

[22] Id. Also sources cited supra, note 43.

[23] The term and approach are coined and proposed in Hockett, *A Fixer-Upper for Finance*, supra note 43.

money chasing too few goods,' one can simply remove some of the relevant money from circulation until the gap is closed. Moreover, like spending, borrowing and, regulating themselves, taxing can be targeted in those sites of spending activity where inflationary pressure is generated.[24] Of course arbitrageurs will seek 'leaks' between targeted and non-targeted subsectors, but this too can be—and often is—regulated.

When 'bubbles' have been generated by credit-fueled speculation on secondary or tertiary financial and derivatives markets, for example, lawyers, economists, and policy-makers have proposed financial transaction or capital gains taxes.[25] Similarly, when spending activity has generated consumer price inflation, value-added (VAT) and other types of taxes have been proposed.[26] Because it is the most overtly 'stick'-like of inflation-fighting measures, the taxation strategy is probably best kept 'in pocket' as only a last resort. It is nevertheless well advised to be mindful of its potential, as a 'backup,' when financing the Green New Deal.

2.2.5 Targeted Open Market Operations

The final two stratagems for dealing with inflationary pressure should it emerge are more innovative and untried than the others. But there have been at least some incipient moves in their direction, the results of which strongly suggest they will work well if employed.

The first such stratagem would generalize Fed open market operations to more assets than Treasury securities, in order to influence more prices than simply money rental prices—that is, interest rates. If, for example, upward price pressures were growing in respect of some systemically important variable like fuel, commodity, or housing costs, or if downward pressures were being placed upon some other important variable like prevailing wages or salaries, public instrumentalities through market activity can apply countervailing pressure. The Fed or another

---

[24] See again Hockett, *Not a Thing*, supra note 43.

[25] See again Hockett, *Fixer-Upper*, supra note 43.

[26] See, for example, Beardsley Ruml (Chairman, Federal Reserve Bank of New York), 'Taxes for Revenue Are Obsolete,' *American Affairs*, January 1946, available at http://home.hiwaay. net/~becraft/RUMLTAXES.html

instrumentality like the National Investment Council (NIC) discussed below, for example, can short-sell the items whose prices are rising, or can 'go long' in the items whose prices are falling.

We might call the full asset portfolio out of which the Fed operates in this manner something like 'The People's Portfolio.'[27] It would effectively function as a full market-mirroring index fund, the composition of which and comparative prices within which the Fed could regularly adjust, in the name of just allocation or price stability, through open market operations.[28]

This is not as exotic a suggestion as might be supposed. When housing prices continued to fall after the 2008 crash, for example, landing more and more homeowners 'underwater' and thus vulnerable to foreclosure and homelessness, the Fed ultimately had to step in to place a 'floor' under still falling home prices. This it did via QE3, pursuant to which it committed, in the autumn of 2012, to purchase at least $85 billion in mortgage-related financial instruments until home prices stabilized. Prices then stabilized within two years of QE3's inception.

Similarly, when speculation in commodity markets, fueled by QE1 and QE2 monetary easing, began to work regressive effects by raising food and commodity prices that non-wealthy Americans in crisis could ill afford, at least one scholar at the New York Fed proposed that the central bank short-sell commodities in order to counteract the ill effects of QE even while retaining the beneficial effects of QE.[29] The job guarantee component of the Green New Deal can be viewed similarly—as a form of 'open labor market operation' aimed at maintaining a living wage economy-wide.[30]

---

[27] See Robert Hockett, *The People's Portfolio: Open Market Operations for Just, Stable Prices*, working paper (2019). Also Robert Hockett & Roy Kreitner, *Just Prices*, 27 Cornell Journal of Law and Public Policy 1 (2018), available at https://papers.ssrn.com/sol3/papers.cfm?abstract_id=3069966

[28] Id.

[29] See Robert Hockett, *How to Make QE More Helpful—By Fed Shorting of Commodities*, Benzinga, Oct. 14, 2011, available at https://www.benzinga.com/news/11/10/1988109/how-to-make-qe-more-helpful-by-fed-shorting-of-commodities

[30] See Robert Hockett, *Open Labor Market Operations*, 62 Challenge 33 (2019), available at https://papers.ssrn.com/sol3/papers.cfm?abstract_id=3298823&fbclid=IwAR25Ti8cwTJ8IsO51 Ja9cekCRHOr51LmYjotYx2Df1W1Mzhqw3AURNw9ROQ

Like more traditional Fed open market operations, these kinds of open market operation are both easily executed and readily justified. One need only highlight the fact that the targeted prices are 'systemically important'—that is, that they pervasively enter into the formation of other prices, are of special significance as a matter of justice, or both.[31]

Economy-wide monetary aggregates and attendant interest rates are obviously significant in this sense, which is precisely why the New York Fed trading desk buys or sells securities each weekday in order to affect them. What remains to be more widely appreciated is that interest rates are not the only prices that are significant in this sense. Financing the Green New Deal, especially given the centrality of justice and the job guarantee to it, should be conducted with full cognizance of the potential offered by additional forms of open market operation.

2.2.6   Fed Taxpayer Wallets and Targeted Interest on Reserves

A final means of heading-off inflationary pressure, should it at some point emerge, would become available if the Fed 'Citizen,' 'Resident,' and 'Government' Wallets proposed below under the heading of 'Taxpayer Wallets' were to be adopted. The idea, more on which shortly, is for the Fed to issue a telephonically or smart-device accessible Democratic Digital Dollar associated with a new system of retail deposit accounts that it will administer for all citizens, firms, and approved residents of the U.S.[32] Currently, only large banking institutions and a favored few other financial conglomerates enjoy the privilege of real time transaction settlement and associated 'Reserve Accounts' at our central bank. These

---

[31] Id.

[32] See Robert Hockett, *A Democratic Digital Dollar: A Peer-to-Peer Savings and Payments Platform for Fully Inclusive State, Local, and National Money and Banking Systems*, 11 Harvard Business Law Journal __ (2019) (forthcoming), available at https://papers.ssrn.com/sol3/papers. cfm?abstract_id=3470931; and Robert Hockett, *Money's Past is Fintech's Future: Wildcat Crypto, the Digital Dollar, and Citizen Central Banking*, 2 Stanford Journal of Blockchain Law & Policy 1 (2019), available at https://papers.ssrn.com/sol3/papers.cfm?abstract_id=3299555. Also Robert Hockett, *Rousseauvian Money*, working paper (2018), available at https://papers.ssrn.com/sol3/ papers.cfm?abstract_id=3278408; Robert Hockett, *The Capital Commons*, working paper (2018); and Robert Hockett & Saule Omarova, *The Citizens' Ledger*, working paper (2019).

accounts yield interest—so-called Interest on Reserves, or IOR—that the Fed is able to use as a monetary policy tool. It can combat inflation by raising IOR, and can combat deflation by lowering IOR—even to 'negative rates' or their functional equivalent if need be.

The theory—or wish—behind IOR is that higher rates on bank Reserve Accounts will translate into higher interest on individual deposit accounts held at the relevant banks, while lower rates on the former will encourage more lending to the latter.[33] Unfortunately, things do not work as intended. Privileged banking institutions do not pass their IOR on to retail deposit holders, nor did lower IOR during the post-2008 era translate into more bank lending as distinguished from bank speculation with cheap Fed-supplied money on commodity markets. This slack in the 'transmission belt' of Fed monetary policy—the 'pushing on a string' problem—is entirely attributable to the presence of Fed-privileged, privately owned banking institutions as 'middlemen' between the citizenry and their central bank.[34]

There are accordingly very good reasons, sounding in both monetary policy efficacy and broader financial inclusion as well as payments system efficiency, to end banks' exclusive access to Fed Reserve Accounting and afford Fed Citizen, Resident, and local Government Wallets, with an associated telephonically usable digital dollar, to all Americans, municipalities, and approved residents. This would allow for Fed 'helicopter drops' directly into the Wallets, along with related 'QE for the People' initiatives, in the event of significant recession or debt-deflation like that of 2008–09, or even 1929–32, in future.[35] It would also allow for a straightforward inflation-fighting measure were that danger ever to loom again: the Fed would simply raise rates paid on Citizen, Resident, and Government Wallets, in either targeted or plenary fashion depending on the nature of the challenge confronting it. Again, there will be more to say on this below.[36]

---

[33] Id.
[34] Id.
[35] Id.
[36] Id.

2.3   Foster Financial and Economic Inclusion

In addition to mobilizing, allocating, and modulating finance capital in pursuit of the Green New Deal goals, a Green New Deal Finance Plan must also work to foster and maintain full financial and broader economic inclusion across the entirety of our population. This justice aspect of the Green New Deal is no mere 'add on' or accidental feature. It lies at the core of the very idea of the Green New Deal.[37]

There are multiple reasons for this, two of which bear special emphasis.

One reason is that the existence of powerless, marginalized communities is virtually a prerequisite to the kind of polluting behavior that has brought our climate to its current precipice. Prosperous, empowered citizens are precisely the ones who are most prompted and able to say 'not in my back yard,' while only the powerless and marginalized can be 'otherized' to the point of enabling the 'externalization' that produces a Flint, Michigan. In a society in which no one is desperately poor enough simply to 'roll over' when confronted by massive pollution, polluters are forced to 'internalize' their own waste—by developing renewable forms of energy and climate mitigation technologies.

A second reason that justice is central to the Green New Deal is that it is precisely the most impoverished and distressed communities that offer most 'bang for the buck' of Green New Deal expenditure at the front end. Those at the lower ends of the income distribution have higher propensities to consume than do other strata, meaning the growth effects of stimulus spending tend to be higher when that spending is first channeled to the presently disadvantaged.[38] Similarly, poorer and traditionally excluded communities tend to be those whose infrastructures and sources of power are most decrepit and polluting, respectively. Hence 'frontloading' our efforts in these communities will tend to yield the most

---

[37] See, for example, House and Senate Resolutions, supra note 1. Also Gunn-Wright & Hockett, *Green New Deal White Paper*, supra note 42; and Hockett, *Pre-Liberal Autonomy and Post-Liberal Finance*, supra note 42.

[38] See generally Robert Hockett & Daniel Dillon, *Income Inequality and Market Fragility: Some Empirics in the Political Economy of Finance*, 62 CHALLENGE 1 (2019), available at https://papers. ssrn.com/sol3/papers.cfm?abstract_id=2204710

immediately dramatic improvements to our infrastructure and climate as well as our economy.[39]

These observations yield some guidelines for the project of financing the Green New Deal.

2.3.1 Channel Finance to Inclusion-Fostering Projects, Subnational Governmental Units, and Private Entities

The first such guideline is already implicit in the foregoing two observations: All else being equal, Green New Deal financial flows should flow first toward projects that will employ the hitherto unemployed, bring choice and opportunity to the hitherto choiceless and hopeless, and bring modernization and abatement to the hitherto run-down and crumbling. This 'preferential option for the least advantaged,' as we might call it, can be exercised in connection with initial choices between projects, between localities, and between project-conducting entities.

2.3.2 Establish Inclusion-Assuring 'Public Options' in Finance

The second guideline derivable from the foregoing observations on inclusion has to do with the development of new financial *institutions* well suited to complement Green New Deal financial *flows*.

2.3.2.1 A 'Peoples' Fed'

One such option has already been mentioned above and is more fully developed below.[40] On the one hand, sizable numbers of our population are unbanked or under-banked. They lack access to garden-variety retail

---

[39] For more on the benefits of frontloading, see Robert Hockett & Robert Frank, *Public Infrastructure Investment, Renewed Economic Growth, and the U.S. Fiscal Position*, 63 CHALLENGE __ (2019) (forthcoming), available at https://papers.ssrn.com/sol3/papers.cfm?abstract_id=1987656
[40] Id.

banking and payment services including deposit accounts, transaction accounts, and small scale credit. On the other hand, we have a gargantuan-sized public banking institution—our Federal Reserve—that provides these services solely to commercial banks and a few other privileged financial institutions. This arrangement is not only unjust, privileging as it does the already most powerful agents in our economy; it is also spectacularly inefficient where payments and the conduct of credit-modulatory monetary policy are concerned, as noted above. It is accordingly desirable to expand citizen and resident access to Federal Reserve banking, along with a telephonically accessible Democratic Digital Dollar, in a manner to be sketched below.

2.3.2.2   Public Banks and Digital Payment Platforms

Another public banking option, which is both complementary to and can be seen as a state or local rendition of the expanded-access Fed just mentioned, is that of public banking patterned more or less after the influential Bank of North Dakota (BND) model that has drawn favorable attention since the 2008 crash. The BND is a not-for-profit, state-administered institution that aims to ensure access to retail banking services and small business, agricultural, and student loans to all residents of its geographic area.[41] It has also worked, successfully, to preserve or restore ownership of homes and other assets to foreclosed owners during times of acute financial distress.

The state of North Dakota uses the BND to conduct all of its own saving, spending, and remittance operations, which provided sufficient 'critical mass' to enable the institution to get up and running quickly from the moment that it was instituted a century ago. Since then it has made North Dakota one of the most financially inclusive states in our union, while also financing multiple state infrastructure projects on reasonable terms that keep the institution 'in the black' without exploiting the state's population.

---

[41] See Bank of North Dakota, *The BND Story*, available at https://bnd.nd.gov/the-bnd-story/. See generally ELLEN BROWN, THE PUBLIC BANKING SOLUTION (2013); and ELLEN BROWN, BANKING ON THE PEOPLE (2019).

For these and other reasons movements have developed across the country to bring public banking to states as far flung and diverse as New York, Pennsylvania, and California, among others. The plan sketched below accordingly integrates a system of state-level public banks with the more federal- and regional-level institutional innovations that it proposes. It also proposes a system of digital public payment platforms and associated 'digital wallets'—what the author calls 'Inclusive Value Ledgers' (IVLs)—that can complement or even substitute for such institutions where necessary.

2.4   Facilitate Democratic Decision-Making and Federalism

Because the Green New Deal aims to maximize public participation by literally everyone pursuant to principles of federalism and subsidiarity (see Sect. 2.3.1), and to allocate financing accordingly, a Green New Deal Finance Plan must also develop broad criteria for the dispersal of funds across 'levels' of government. We can think of this as funding that respects a kind of jurisdictional division of labor among our public instrumentalities. That is, it will allocate funds to differing units of government in keeping with their comparative advantages.

2.4.1   Federal Government's Comparative Advantage: Maximal Coordination Capacity, Plenary Regulatory Jurisdiction, Public Full Faith and Credit

As noted above, the federal government's key comparative strengths are its capacity to coordinate efforts nationwide, to use its plenary jurisdiction when necessary to ensure that Green New Deal efforts remain in conformity to our Constitution and laws, and to deploy its maximal full faith and credit to ensure adequate funding flows to all parts of the country that need it.

The importance of the first of these strengths is obvious. As noted several times above, optimizing the Green New Deal requires that multiple regional, state, and local efforts are mutually complementary and not mutually undercutting. Only our federal government has that capacity. This same level of government also is the only one with sufficiently broad legal authority to ensure such mutual complementarity.

Finally, as the issuer both of the national currency and of the only form of sovereign debt for which there is deep demand worldwide—at some $20 trillion, the market for Treasurys is by far the world's largest financial market—our federal government is by far the best financially resourced instrumentality we have. This in turn means that our federal government can ensure that funds flow not only to already affluent sectors and regions of the country, but also to those that are less advantaged. In the final analysis, this is what a 'fiscal union' such as the U.S. is all about.[42]

2.4.2   Local Government's Comparative Advantage: Direct Responsiveness to Local Needs, Preferences, and Decisions ('Participatory Budgeting'); Some (Limited) Financing Capacity

As noted above, local governments' strengths and weaknesses are the mirror image of the federal government's. On the one hand, they are much closer, hence responsive and accountable, to their constituents than are other levels of government. On the other hand, their financial capacities are the most constrained. The Green New Deal should accordingly foster, encourage, and support Green New Deal project selection and 'participatory budgeting' at the local level, while affording all requisite funding assistance from the federal level. The latter, as effectively suggested above and more fully developed below, can take many forms—from direct

---

[42] See Robert Hockett, 'What the Euro's Current Difficulties Really Mean,' *The Hill*, July 4, 2015, available at https://thehill.com/blogs/pundits-blog/international/246834-what-the-euros-current-difficulties-really-mean. Also Robert Hockett, 'Save Europe's Marriage with a Trial Separation,' *Bloomberg*, June 12, 2012, available at https://www.bloomberg.com/opinion/articles/2012-06-12/save-europe-s-marriage-with-a-trial-separation

grants through loans all the way to accommodative purchases of locally issued financial instruments.

2.4.2.1 State and Regional Governments' Comparative Advantage: Coordination Intermediate Between Federal and Local Governments; Some Intermediate-Level Financing Capacity As Well

Against the backdrop just provided, the appropriate role of state governments and modes of subnational, regional compacts among states is that of an intermediating link between federal and local levels of government. Indeed, some states have greater financial capacity than others, while all states have representation in the U.S. Senate complementary to that of their Congressional Districts in the U.S. House of Representatives. The states can accordingly play an important role in optimizing the allocation of Green New Deal funding across literally all of the nation's distinct localities.

2.5 Ensure an Optimal Division of Labor Between Public and Private Sectors

As noted above (see Sect. 2.3.2), a Green New Deal Finance Plan should also operate in keeping with an optimal division of labor as between 'public' and 'private' sectors of organized productive activity. Here too, as in the case of different levels of government, this means allocation that optimally levers distinct sectors' comparative advantages.

2.5.1 Public's Comparative Advantage: Democratic Accountability, Regulatory Jurisdiction, Financial Capacity

The public sector's strengths are its democratic accountability, jurisdictional authority and, especially in the case of our federal government, its financial capacities. If, for example, one impediment to the broad

popularization of electric vehicles is the absence of charging ports at parking meters, there is an obstacle faced by the privately owned manufacturers and sellers of such vehicles that the latter have no authority to remove.

A state or local government, on the other hand, has this authority even
while lacking capacity in our market economy to manufacture and sell
such vehicles. The obvious solution to this problem is to wed public sector jurisdictional capacity with private sector manufacturing capacity,
with the former either directly supplying or contracting for installation of
charging ports at parking meters and the latter producing and selling the
vehicles whose drivers can then use those ports.

This example also makes for a good opportunity to appreciate the role
of coordination and its facilitation among not only public and private,
but also distinct levels of government in the Green New Deal:

It might, for example, make little sense for a manufacturer to produce
y rather than x electric vehicles, with y greater than x, absent some assurance that there will be charging stations at some localities' parking
meters. It might also make little sense for this manufacturer to produce
z electric vehicles, with z greater than y, absent some assurance that there
will be charging stations at parking meters in *multiple* localities.
Meanwhile, it will make little sense for localities, states, or the federal
government to take measures facilitating the wide use of electric vehicles
absent any assurance that people will buy them and manufacturers will
produce them.

The obvious solution to this 'Alphonse and Gaston' ('after you,' 'no,
after you'[43]) problem is for private producers and various levels of government to coordinate. The former can conduct the market research showing potential demand for electric vehicles in the event that a complementary
public infrastructure is put into place. Local governments then can put
that infrastructure into place, if need be with assistance or inducements
from state governments and financing assistance from the federal government. In this sense the imagined transition to an electric vehicle economy
can be likened to a symphony as distinguished from a cacophony, with

---

[43] Alphonse and Gaston were a popular pair of American cartoon characters in the early twentieth
century. See 'Alphonse and Gaston,' *Revolvy*, available at https://www.revolvy.com/page/
Alphonse-and-Gaston

each party doing what it does best in coordination with the other parties instead of each playing its own tune on its own instrument and the whole thereby producing only discordant noise.

2.5.2 Private Sector's Comparative Advantage: Some Accountability and Responsiveness to Consumer Demand, Some Information-Aggregative Capacity in the Form of Investment Demand with Respect to Specific Firms or Projects

As in effect just noted, the private sector's comparative advantages stem largely from the fact that ours is a 'mixed' market economy. Under our market arrangement, private owned entities produce most of our manufactures and provide many of our desired services. This in turn 'democratizes' them up to a point, inasmuch as it subjects them, at least in the absence of monopoly or oligopoly, to consumer demand and 'incentivizes' them to conduct market research so as to discern such demand.

Where there are also markets for firms' financial securities, moreover, it is possible to ascertain market analysts' informed judgments as to firms'—and hence their products' or services'—future prospects. For the industry of financial analysts informs institutional investors of those prospects for a fee—such is their business model—whereupon those investors buy or sell firms' securities in view of those prospects. The upshot, at least in the medium-to-long term, is that securities prices supply valuable 'price information' that can be taken into account by public and private sector Green New Deal planners in deciding where to allocate funds.[44]

---

[44] This potential 'price discovery' function of the markets is familiar to financial theory, and can be put at the service of public planning if the latter is done thoughtfully. The plan laid out in Chap. 3 will show how. For further background, see, for example, 'Price Discovery,' *Investopedia*, available at https://www.investopedia.com/terms/p/pricediscovery.asp. Also Robert Hockett, *Real Arrow Securities for All: Just and Efficient Insurance Through Macro-Hedging*, 34 Rᴇᴠ. Bᴀɴᴋɪɴɢ & Fɪɴ. Lᴀᴡ 1 (2014), available at https://papers.ssrn.com/sol3/papers.cfm?abstract_id=2435781

3

A Green New Deal Financial Architecture

The Green New Deal's financial flows and financial architecture should be as responsive as possible to the considerations elaborated immediately above. The institutions and institutional reforms proposed below are developed with all of them firmly in view. The summary version is this: With (a) the establishment of one new federal instrumentality of a kind that the U.S. has had before, and (b) two complementary reforms to an institution we already have, a full Green New Deal financing architecture can be put into place with only minimal 'tweaking' of existing institutional arrangements.

The new institution is a National Investment Council, which amounts to a contemporary rendition of Alexander Hamilton's Bank of the United States, Woodrow Wilson's War Finance Corporation, and Herbert Hoover and Franklin Roosevelt's Reconstruction Finance Corporation.[1] The existing institution is our Federal Reserve System, which continues to bear much of the structure and mandate it has borne since its founding

---

[1] See sources cited supra, note 35. It also bears some similarity to the Board of National Investments (BNI) proposed by J.M. Keynes and, to a lesser degree, the free-standing National Investment authority proposed by this author and Professor Omarova in 2015 and 2017. See id.; see also J.M. KEYNES ET AL., BRITAIN'S INDUSTRIAL FUTURE (1928), and infra, note 81.

© The Author(s) 2020
R. C. Hockett, *Financing the Green New Deal,*
https://doi.org/10.1007/978-3-030-48450-7_3

in 1913—a structure and mandate now due for an upgrade. These reforms are sequentially elaborated below. Also elaborated is a means of 'building up' to full federal reform from local, state, and regional reforms that can complement or even catalyze the national renewal envisaged here.

3.1   National Investment Council

In order to ensure optimal coordination among (a) the 14 Green New Deal Project Fields, (b) the multiple levels and units of government involved in realizing the Green New Deal, and (c) the public and private sector entities also involved in realizing the Green New Deal, it will be necessary to establish a coordinative council charged with the task of overseeing and facilitating the project's many activities. In view of its structural similarities to the Financial Stability Oversight Council (FSOC), which aggregates information for and coordinates efforts among the nation's multiple *finance-regulatory* agencies, we can call this new institution a 'National Investment Council' (NIC, or Council).[2]

The NIC will effectively constitute a partial contemporary analogue to both (a) the War Finance Corporation (WFC) that oversaw and coordinated our national mobilization effort during the First World War, and (b) the Reconstruction Finance Corporation (RFC) that oversaw and coordinated first the New Deal, then the Second World War mobilization efforts. It will also bear similarities to the First Bank of the United States, designed by the nation's first Treasury Secretary, Alexander Hamilton, to coordinate and facilitate our then-new nation's financial and economic development.[3]

---

[2] For more on the FSOC, its animating considerations and ongoing functions, see Hockett, *Macroprudential Turn*, supra note 11. See also Robert Hockett, Oversight of the Financial Stability Oversight Council: Due Process and Transparency in Non-Bank SIFI Designations, Testimony Before the U.S. House Committee on Financial Services, November 19, 2015, available at https://financialservices.house.gov/uploadedfiles/11.19.2015_robert_hockett_testimony.pdf

[3] These histories are fully elaborated in McDonald, Alexander Hamilton, supra note 35; Hockett, *Post-Liberal Finance*, supra note 35; Jesse H. Jones, Fifty Billion Dollars: My Thirteen Years with the RFC (1951); Robert Hockett & Saule Omarova, *Private Wealth and Public Goods: A Case for a National Investment Authority*, 43 Journal of Corporate Law 101 (2018); and Robert Hockett & Saule Omarova, *Public Actors in Private Markets: Toward a Development Finance State*, 93 Washington University Law Review 103 (2015). See also Keynes

Indeed, one way to explain our nation's present travails is by reference to our having forgotten that 'development' and 'reconstruction' are never finished or 'done deals.' They are never 'completed' or 'accomplished' tasks, any more than are knowledge, science, technology, or history. Like technology itself, national economies are forever developing, forever self-renewing, forever 'upgrading.' The NIC proposed here is designed as much with that truth in view as it is with the desiderata elaborated above in Chap. 2 in view. It is aimed both at optimizing the unavoidable process of national renewal and revitalization which the Green New Deal ultimately is, and at ensuring perpetual upgrading and renewal going forward.

3.1.1 Role and Functions, 'Level' of Government

The NIC will bear primary responsibility for developing and pursuing the Green New Deal at the federal level. This will involve planning and coordinating in collaboration with other federal agencies, other levels of government, and the private sector—just as was done by Hamilton's First Bank of the United States, the WFC, and the RFC during earlier periods of our history. The Council will also coordinate and in many cases secure or provide funding for the many projects that will make up the Green New Deal. This it can do partly with congressionally appropriated funds and partly with bond issuances as well as, going forward, returns on its own investments—again as was done by its predecessors.[4]

Where securing or providing funding is concerned, the Council will have multiple options. It can lend directly to, or purchase equity stakes in or bonds issued by, targeted entities or enterprises. It can also do so for syndicates of financiers, including private sector ones, that it itself forms. Or it can recommend *Fed* purchases of such issuances. As for its own funding, at the front end this can come through either or both Congressional appropriations and bond sales of its own. The latter in turn can include general purpose instruments, sector-specific

---

ET AL., id. The NIC elaborated here can be interpreted as a more FSOC-reminiscent 'streamlined' rendition of the more complex NIA developed in the latter two articles, as well as a contemporary American analogue of Keynes's BNI.

[4] See again sources cited supra, note 80.

instruments, and even project-specific instruments. Going the latter route can enable the Council in effect to employ markets' 'price discovery' mechanisms to acquire preliminary information as to the likely success or otherwise of particular contemplated projects.[5] Going forward, as NIC investments begin yielding returns as did Bank of the United States and RFC investments in their eras, the NIC can plow those return into further investments, generating a longer-term positive 'snowball' effect.

The Council will work closely with the private sector in the grand project of greenifying the national economy, and this in turn will involve bringing together the operations of many now-diffuse federal instrumentalities—many of which used to operate within one structure in the past when they were RFC subsidiaries. It is easy to imagine the potential for thereby establishing a more seamlessly integrated network of public-private venture capital and small business financing operations. Various federal venture capital funds and other federal agencies and programs targeting innovative start-ups—such as, for example, the Telecommunications Development Fund (TDF)[6] and the Small Business Administration (SBA)[7]—can be organizationally incorporated into the NIC structure just as they previously were in the RFC structure.

As suggested above, the Council will also work in particularly close collaboration with the Fed, the Department of the Treasury, and the specific cabinet level departments of the federal government whose mandates embrace specific Green New Deal Project Fields. The reason for close collaboration with Fed and Treasury is that the NIC's financial and fiscal operations will be adjacent to—and indeed operationally situated between and thus unavoidably interactive with—those of these two entities, respectively, and hence must be conducted in harmony with them. The reason for close collaboration with other cabinet level units of federal

---

[5] See again supra, note 78, and associated text.

[6] TDF is a federal venture capital fund created in 1996 for the general purpose of financing small businesses developing telecommunications technologies. See 47 U.S.C. 614 (2015). TDF's strategy focuses on equity investments in telecommunications start-ups. See, S. Jenell Trigg, *Telecommunications Development Fund: Making a Difference?* (2002), available at http://www.civil-rights.org/publications/1996_telecommunications/section-714.html

[7] SBA was established in 1953 to facilitate small business formation and growth via the so-called three Cs of capital, contracting, and counseling. See *About the SBA*, U.S. SMALL BUS. ADMIN., https://www.sba.gov/category/navigation-structure/about-sba

governance, in turn, is that the Green New Deal Project Fields in many cases fall within the functional mandates of the corresponding departments—much as particular pieces of the New Deal and Second World War mobilizations before them did.

The Green New Deal's efforts in the realm of transport infrastructure, for example, implicate the work of the Department of Transportation (DOT). Its efforts in the realm of energy infrastructures similarly implicate the work of the Department of Energy (DOE). Its efforts in the realm of pollution abatement and environmental cleanup, in turn, implicate the work of the Environmental Protection Agency (EPA) and the Department of the Interior (DOI), while its administering of any Green New Deal employment programs will implicate the work of the Department of Labor (DOL), the National Labor Relations Board (NLRB), and the Equal Employment Opportunity Commission (EEOC). Insofar as the NIC works to facilitate the establishment of 'green startup' companies in the private sector, meanwhile, it will implicate the work of the aforementioned TDF and SBA.

In all of these and in other Project Fields, it will be critical that the NIC on the one hand and other cabinet level departments on the other not operate at crossed-purposes. It will also be important not to waste or overlook the considerable expertise, and the many collaborative relations with other levels and units of government as well as private sector industries, that these departments have developed over the decades. Much as the FSOC acts as a coordinating body among Treasury, Fed, the Securities and Exchange Commission (SEC), the Commodity Futures Trading Commission (CFTC), the Federal Deposit Insurance Corporation (FDIC), and other financial regulators, so should the NIC do in collaboration with *its* mandate participants.

3.1.2   Structure, Governance, Relations with Private Sector and Other Levels and Units of Government

There are many ways in which the NIC might be composed, structured, and both internally and externally governed. One attractive prospect is to think of the NIC as a 'system,' by analogy with the Federal Reserve System, and to adopt either a three- or a four-tiered structure along the following lines.

3.1.2.1   Tier One: The Council

The *first* option for the top tier would be the heads of the various departments and other agencies mentioned above, whose fields of expertise and mandates overlap with or are adjacent to those of the NIC itself. This can be thought of as a sort of oversight and strategic planning board, comparable to the FSOC as noted above and to the Board of Governors of the Federal Reserve System.[8] It can accordingly be called 'the Council,' as the FSOC is called, and as the Fed Board of Governors is called 'the Board.'

Ideally, the Council will make decisions in a consensual manner, with voting conducted pursuant to the majority-rule principle only when consensus proves impossible to reach. This, too, would largely replicate FSOC and Fed practice.[9] It probably makes sense for the Council to be chaired by a distinct person, appointed by the President for, say, seven-year terms with the advice and consent of the Senate. This would follow Fed practice, though the seven-year terms would of course exceed the four-year terms of Fed Chairs.

An alternative possibility is to make the Treasury Secretary herself the chair, as is done in the case of FSOC.[10] The advantage offered by this mode of operation is its subjecting the Council to more direct presidential control. But this can also operate as a disadvantage, inasmuch as the investment horizons of the NIC must be long, and accordingly not overly vulnerable to sudden changes in politically sensitive presidential administration.

In the final analysis, because the NIC will in effect be functionally and operationally situated midway between the quite independent Fed and the less independent Treasury, it probably makes sense to confer upon it a degree of independence intermediate between those of the Fed and the

---

[8] See again Hockett, sources cited supra, note 80.
[9] Id.
[10] Id.

Treasury. Appointing a separate chair for seven-year terms—longer than those of Treasury secretaries and Fed chairs, while shorter than the 14-year terms of other Fed Board Governors—seems sensible against that backdrop. Changes can be legislated in future should seven-year terms come to seem too brief or too lengthy.

Similar considerations to those recommending seven-year terms might also militate in favor of appointing additional independent members to the Council, as a means of lessening the degree of dependence on the White House that the present FSOC model entails.[11] In the alternative, the Council might be made to comprise only independent members appointed by the President for staggered seven- or ten-year terms with the advice and consent of the Senate, after the manner of the Federal Reserve Board (FRB). Under this scenario, which we can call the *second* option for the top tier, the other agency and department heads mentioned above—those of the DOT, DOE, DOL, and so on—would be empaneled on an Advisory or Coordination Board, with authority only to make recommendations to, not actually control, the Council.

In the event that this more independent, FRB-reminiscent governance model is adopted, it would make sense to choose Council Governors on the basis of criteria analogous to those used in choosing Fed Board Governors. A 7- or 14-member Council might then be assembled, its members possessed both of expertise in the 14 Green New Deal Project Fields and past experience in government, industry, the academy, or some combination of these. In essence, the idea would be for the Council's membership to be diversified in a manner mirroring the diversity of the Green New Deal itself, which as noted implicates 14 Project fields, multiple levels of government, and private as well as public sector entities.

3.1.2.2   Tier Two: The Investment Committee

Whichever option for the NIC's top tier we adopt, it probably makes sense to impanel just below it a more operationally focused tier. It would be at this level that more detailed planning and execution of

---

[11] Id.

project-specific NIC financing is done. We might call this the NIC Investment Committee, and think of its role in rough analogy to the Open Market Committee of the Fed (FOMC), the finance committee of any large business concern possessed of a chief financial officer (CFO), or the investment or fund manager of any investment bank or investment fund.

The Investment Committee under this scenario would assess and develop various financing options for various Green New Deal projects or portfolios of such projects, with appropriations, retained earnings, or bond sales on the income side and running from grants through loans to bond purchases and equity investments on the output side, all in conformity with the goals and desiderata elaborated above in Chap. 2. It would then present these options to the Council for approval or selection, then execute on whatever options the Council ultimately opts for.

The Investment Committee might comprise a simple subcommittee of the Council itself, again partly reminiscent of the Fed FOMC model, or might comprise mainly or only persons with significant financial management experience, with the chair of the Commission itself also serving as chair, ex officio or otherwise, of the Committee. Either way, in view of the mainly technical nature of its functions, the Committee members should have, jointly and severally, top level financial expertise and experience. For the Committee will, in effect, be conducting the NIC's principal funding and investment operations like any finance committee or investment or fund manager.

One additional layer of possible nuance is worth noting: It might be well to subdivide the Investment Committee into two subcommittees, one concerned primarily with direct 'primary' market investment, the other concerned with indirect, secondary and tertiary market operations. In such case the Primary Market Subcommittee would act much like a contemporary infrastructure bank does in underwriting and capital-raising more generally. The Secondary Market Subcommittee, analogously, would function more like a fund manager in purchasing various kinds of securities issued by private and public sector entities whose investment operations complement the Council's mandate.

Needless to say, both subcommittees would coordinate, as the departments of any complex institution do, under the auspices of the Investment

Committee of which they are part. And the latter Committee, as noted above, would operate under the continuous oversight of the Council.

3.1.2.3   Tier Three: The Regional NIC Banks

The third tier of the NIC System would be a cluster of regional banks, perhaps roughly patterned after the Fed system of regional Federal Reserve Banks. The idea behind this arrangement would be to afford the federal instrumentality in question 'eyes,' 'ears,' and operational capacity in regions of the country whose primary industries and economic conditions differ from one another in nontrivial ways. The Federal Reserve Bank of New York (FRBNY), for example, has expertise in and jurisdiction over much of the nation's financial services industry, which is of course largely headquartered in New York. The Federal Reserve Bank of Dallas, by contrast, has more expertise in energy and agriculture, in keeping with its region's primary industries. It makes sense for the NIC to operate out of regional locations that are similarly sensitive to regionally varying economies and infrastructure needs.

The Fed regional structure was developed over a century ago, when the nation's economy was less fully integrated than it is now and its regional economic profiles were in some ways quite different from what they have developed into since. This presents something of a dilemma where regionally structuring the NIC's third tier is concerned. On the one hand, in view of the close coordinating that the NIC will have to do with the Fed, it makes some sense for the NIC's regional structure to mirror that of the Fed itself. On the other hand, because the latter structure has grown somewhat anachronistic in light of regional conditions' many changes since 1913, to mirror the Fed would be to 'lock in' the same now-anachronistic division of regional labor at the NIC.

The optimal solution here would probably be to reapportion the Fed's regional Reserve Banks in keeping with contemporary regional conditions (not by 'reshuffling' from east to west, but by adding *new* regional Federal Reserve Banks out west), and then to apportion the NIC's regional banks isomorphically. Short of that, the best option would likely be to arrange the NIC's regional divisions as we would wish to do with the Fed under contemporary conditions. Then, where these do not coincide with established regional Federal Reserve Banks, the NIC Banks can coordinate with *local offices* of regional Fed Reserve Banks. These latter exist in some bundance, as they represent the Fed's own response to the regional changes that have unfolded over the last century.

However we decide to structure the NIC's regional layer of distinct NIC Banks, it probably makes sense for their roles and internal governance structures to follow a pattern that slightly varies on those of their Fed analogues. The ideal arrangement would probably be classified boards with one class of directors chosen by the NIC, another by affected state and local governments, and a third by regionally important industries and labor organizations—all subject to NIC veto as in the case of the Fed. The function of the regional banks would then be to 'interface' with subnational units of government, industry, and labor in their regions for purposes of both communication and finance allocation. In this connection, a particularly important role of the regional NIC Banks will be to work in collaboration with the system of 'public banks' elaborated below. And now that the Fed has opened a new Municipal Liquidity Facility to assist with state and local financing needs in the face of the spring 2020 Coronavirus pandemic, another such role might be to liaise between regional Federal Reserve Banks on the one hand, and states and municipalities aiming to build infrastructural capacity quickly while using the new facility on the other hand.[12]

3.1.3   Pictorial Representation

Figure 3.1 depicts the components, organizational structure, and financial flows associated with the NIC. Line segments represent administrative linkage, while arrows indicate financial flows. 'Appropriations' means

---

[12] For more on the new MLF, see, for example, Robert Hockett, *Community QE: Key Provisions and a 'Game Plan' for Immediate State Action*, available at https://papers.ssrn.com/sol3/papers. cfm?abstract_id=3574157. Also Robert Hockett, 'Community QE: An April Game Plan for States and Cities,' *Forbes*, April 12, 2020, available at https://www.forbes.com/sites/rhockett/2020/04/12/community-qean-april-game-plan-for-states-and-cities/#138495c03624; and Robert Hockett, 'Welcome to Community QE: Now Let Us Put It to Use,' *Forbes*, April 9, 2020, available at https://www.forbes.com/sites/rhockett/2020/04/09/welcome-to-community-qe/#1e84d9fcc415.   For more establing additional regional Federal Reserve Banks, see Robert Hockett, *Spread the Fed: Distributed Central Banking in Pandemic and Beyond*, 14 Virginia Law and Business Review __ (2020) (forthcoming).

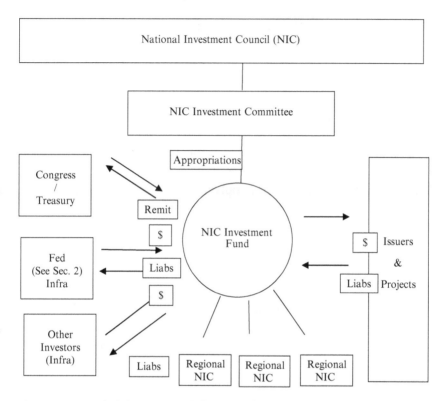

Fig. 3.1 NIC administrative and financial flow structure. (Source: Author's creation)

congressionally appropriated funds, 'remittances' means possible remittances to Treasury, 'Liabs' means financial liabilities (i.e., payment obligations),' and '$' means money payment.

It should be noted that if the division of the Investment Committee into distinct Primary Market and Secondary Market Subcommittees suggested above is adopted, the NIC Investment Fund depicted in Fig. 3.1 will be correspondingly bifurcated. There might, indeed, be multiple funds, according as the Committee judges prudent in pursuing multiple public investment avenues or strategies. This too would be a structure familiar to contemporary finance, in effect constituting a public sector analogue to the 'family of funds' model found in the investment company (especially 'open end' mutual fund) industry.

3.2   Federal Reserve Reforms

As discussed in Chap. 2 above, a key component of the Green New Deal is its focus on broad financial and economic inclusion on the part of our entire population. This is partly a matter of democratic justice and redress for past wrongs to distinct segments of our population.[13] It is likewise partly a matter of optimizing, in respect of both equitable benefit-distribution and macroeconomic stability-maintenance, the way in which the Green New Deal is executed over the coming decade. The Green New Deal succeeds only if the full population is 'on board' with it, actively involved in the planning, the executing, and the benefitting. This militates strongly in favor of certain Fed reforms that will make of the Fed a full partner of and complement to the National Investment Council in advancing the Green New Deal and its transformative objectives.

3.2.1   A 'Peoples' Fed' and 'Democratic Digital Dollar'

A key role in providing for broad participation in the name of both justice and stability as the Green New Deal unfolds will be played by the system of digitized Fed (or Treasury) Taxpayer Wallets mentioned in Chap. 2 and is elaborated below. We can think of these reforms as means of converting the Fed from an old-fashioned 'bank to the banks,' as it is now, to a modern and state-of-the-art 'bank of the people,' which is more consonant both with our nation's founding ideals and with the goals of the Green New Deal.[14]

It is also a means of minimizing the degree to which Green New Deal needs to 'reinvent the wheel.' For it adapts an already existing federal instrumentality—the Fed—to circumstances that have changed quite dramatically since the Fed's founding in 1913, and does so in a way, as will now be described, that simply carries forth a developmental

---

[13] See again sources cited supra, note 38, and associated text.
[14] See again sources cited supra, note 66, and associated text.

trajectory that the Fed's current operations, as these have evolved over the past century, already display.[15]

3.2.1.1   Fundamental Idea and Prompting Considerations

The People's Fed and Democratic Digital Dollar idea, as suggested in Chap. 2, is a means of furthering the Green New Deal's inclusion objectives while also affording the citizenry a direct financial 'stake' in the massive degree of wealth-generation that the Green New Deal will occasion. It is also a means of rationalizing and speeding up the nation's payments system and supplying an ideal mechanism for the maintenance of price stability as the Green New Deal unfolds, again in keeping with the goals discussed above in Chap. 2.

Mechanically speaking, the core idea here is very simple. It is for the Fed, perhaps following the Treasury in the way to be described below, to issue a digital dollar and to afford every citizen, firm, unit of government, and any approved non-citizen resident, a digitized and device-accessible deposit-cum-transaction 'wallet' denominated in that dollar. These will function essentially as demand deposit accounts privately held at commercial banks, and Fed 'Reserve Accounts' maintained on behalf of banks and other privileged financial institutions at the Fed, do now. But they will be digital wallets accessible and usable anywhere through smartphones and similar devices.

This new system will facilitate telephonic banking and immediate clearing of transactions on the liability side of the Fed's balance sheet.[16] It will also immediately offer both the Green New Deal and the nation more broadly a plethora of additional benefits that are long overdue. We can reprise these briefly, then sketch out a bit more operational detail.

---

[15] This trajectory is more fully elaborated in Hockett, *Rousseauvian Money*, supra note 66; and Hockett, *The Capital Commons*, supra note 66.
[16] Id.

3.2.1.1.1   Inclusion

The first benefit will be an immediate end to the pervasive degree of financial exclusion and, with it, economic marginalization that presently characterizes the nation's commercial payments system, financial system, and broader economy.[17] Gone in one stroke will be the chronic American problem of the 'unbanked' and 'underbanked,' which not only deprives the nation of the productive talents and creativity of literally scores of millions among us, but also unjustly subjects the marginalized to the depredations of 'payday lenders,' 'check-cashers,' and other species of 'rent-seeker' and 'loan shark.'[18]

3.2.1.1.2   'Direct' Monetary Policy: a.k.a. 'QE for the People'

The second benefit of a People's Fed and Democratic Digital Dollar will be a far more effective channel for the conduct of counter-inflationary and counter-deflationary Fed monetary policy as described above in Chap. 2. The present monetary policy 'transmission belt,' as it is called, is subject to profoundly wasteful leakages. For it relies indispensably on 'middleman' institutions that mediate between the taxpayers on the one hand and their central bank on the other hand.[19]

Expansionary policy during a recession, for example, relies on privately owned banks to lend cheap federal funds to individuals and businesses; yet these banks frequently use the funds simply to speculate on commodity and other markets, thereby routing funds away from their intended recipients and toward endeavors that actually raise the prices of

---

[17] See again sources cited supra, notes 42 and 66, and accompanying text. Also ROBERT HOCKETT, CHAKA'S WINDOWS: WORKS AND DAYS IN THE LIFE OF A 'HOMELESS ENTREPRENEUR' (2019) (book manuscript, on file with the author). Also Robert Hockett, *A Democratic Digital Dollar: A Peer-to-Peer Savings and Payments Platform for Fully Inclusive State, Local, and National Money and Banking Systems*, 11 HARVARD BUSINESS LAW JOURNAL __ (2019) (forthcoming), available at https://papers.ssrn.com/sol3/papers.cfm?abstract_id=3470931

[18] See generally Robert Hockett, 'Sanders and Occasio-Cortez Offer Real "Financial Choice" with Their Loanshark Prevention Act,' *Forbes*, May 13, 2019, available at https://www.forbes.com/sites/rhockett/2019/05/13/sanders-and-ocasio-cortez-offer-real-financial-choice/#74e793d33c84. Also Hockett, *Democratic Digital Dollar*, id.

[19] See again sources cited supra, note 66, and associated text.

necessities that ordinary citizens must purchase—foodstuffs and fuel, for example.[20]

'Direct' taxpayer/central-bank banking will sidestep these leakages. Counter-deflationary monetary policy, for example, can be effected through direct crediting of Fed Taxpayer Wallets—in effect, a sort of 'QE for the People' or digital 'citizen helicopter money' far more effective, and just, than the forms of QE and helicopter drop employed during the Great Recession only a few years ago.[21] Counter-inflationary policy, for its part, can be effected simply by raising interest on Taxpayer Wallets—the analogue to IOR currently enjoyed by privileged banking institutions with Fed Reserve Accounts—thereby boosting the attractiveness of saving over spending to individuals when this is macro-economically desirable.[22]

3.2.1.1.3   Credit Modulation and Allocation

Similarly, the system of digital Fed Taxpayer Wallets will allow for far more effective credit modulation and allocation than is presently possible.[23] Modulation will be effected through the newly leak-proof monetary policy transmission belt as just described. Allocation, in turn, can be conducted via the same mechanism. A particular firm, industry, state, municipality, or other entity that the NIC approves for funding in pursuit of one or another Green New Deal project, for example, can receive those funds directly in its Fed Taxpayer Wallet. That can take the form of a transfer from a Treasury Account, an NIC Account, or some other account also maintained by the Fed.[24]

---

[20] See again sources cited supra, notes 63 and 66, and associated text.

[21] Id.

[22] Id.

[23] See again sources cited supra, note 66, and associated text.

[24] Id.

3.2.1.1.4   Modernize Payments and Steer 'Fintech' in Green New Deal-Friendly Directions

A final benefit offered by a new system of Fed Taxpayer Wallets and associated Democratic Digital Dollar will be the opportunity it affords both to modernize the national payments system and to steer the many new financial technologies now discussed under the heading of 'fintech' in salutary, socially beneficial directions. New blockchain and distributed ledger technologies, along with the digital currencies associated with them, are of course now undergoing a 'revolution' of sorts in their development and proliferation.[25] This development, affecting as it does those public utilities which are the nation's payments and financial systems, should not be left to chance or to rent-seeking behavior. It should be guided by the populace in keeping with our national needs.

Many of the claims made for the new financial technologies by their enthusiasts are breathless and, in some cases, even ridiculous.[26] Some of these technologies definitely have the potential to change the financial landscape for good or for ill, however, and many of the world's central banks are accordingly now actively experimenting with some of the relevant technologies as they look to upgrade their national payments systems and facilitate digital banking and transacting.[27] Furthest along thus far is Sweden, whose 'e-Krona' project went online, on a trial basis, in February of 2020.[28]

Against this backdrop, a Fed-administered digital dollar looks all but inevitable.[29] And this actually can aid in the project of affording greater financial inclusion. For a system of Fed-administered Citizen, Resident, and Government Wallets then could be accessed by their users not only

---

[25] See again Hockett, *Fintech's Future*, supra note 66; Hockett, *Capital Commons*, supra note 66; Hockett, *Democratic Digital Dollar*, supra note 89. Also Robert Hockett, 'Facebook's Proposed Crypto-Currency—More Pisces than Libra for Now,' *Forbes*, June 20, 2019, available at https://www.forbes.com/sites/rhockett/2019/06/20/facebooks-proposed-crypto-currency-more-pisces-than-libra-for-now/#5dbe692d2be2; and Robert Hockett, *Digital Greenbacks*, 72 Administrative Law Review __ (2020) (forthcoming).

[26] Id.

[27] Id.

[28] Id.

[29] Id.

online or at ATMs and teller windows, but also via smartphones and similar devices.[30]

Many underdeveloped countries with past histories of undeveloped banking sectors already are 'leapfrogging' into the twenty-first century, skipping over the twentieth, with phone-banking technologies.[31] There is no reason the U.S. can't do likewise on behalf of the banked and unbanked. And the Fed's expansion of its system of Reserve Accounts to embrace Taxpayer Wallets would afford an opportune moment to do so.[32]

The proposal below will accordingly take the form of a system of digitized, telephonically usable Fed Taxpayer Wallets, the currency of which will be what we might call a Democratic Digital Dollar.

3.2.1.2   Accounting and Operational Dynamics

Operationally speaking, the transition to a full 'People's Fed' will occur in two stages. Each stage will visit its own effects upon the Fed balance sheet—that is, its book of liabilities and its asset portfolio. The second stage, moreover, will also make of the Fed a seamlessly integrated complement to the NIC as described above.[33]

During the first stage, private bank deposit liabilities to depositors will simply convert into discount window liabilities owed to the Fed. Banks' asset portfolios will be unchanged. In effect, the Fed will simply be interposed between depositors and commercial banks, with the Fed owing those whom the banks previously owed, and the banks owing the Fed instead of the depositors.[34]

During the second stage, as people begin themselves making deposits into their digital Fed Taxpayer Wallets—even deposits, such as paychecks and benefit checks, that are not loan proceeds—the Fed will begin to hold more and more assets that are not simply discount window loans

---

[30] Id.

[31] Id.

[32] Id.

[33] Fuller elaboration is available in Hockett, *Capital Commons*, supra note 66; Hockett, *Democratic Digital Dollar*, supra note 89; and Hockett & Omarova, *The Citizens' Ledger*, supra note 66.

[34] Id.

made to commercial banks. Now there will also be NIC and NIC-recommended securities as described above, and securities held in the Price Stabilization Fund (or People's Portfolio) described below.[35]

One long-term change that this switch will make to 'the business of *banking*' is worth noting here too, as it represents a salutary 'side benefit.'[36] Insofar as privately owned banks continue to lend in ways that find expression in the form of newly opened deposits, the latter will have to be deposited into Fed Taxpayer Wallets, meaning in turn that the banks will have to borrow through the Fed discount window.[37] This presents a welcome opportunity to the public for purposes of money modulation and credit allocation as described above in Chap. 2. For the Fed already conditions discount window lending upon financed assets' possessing certain socially desirable characteristics. It can now *add* conditions that further its evolving modulatory and allocative mission—rather as Government Sponsored Enterprises (GSEs) such as Fannie Mae have historically limited their secondary market making activities to so-called 'conforming loans.'[38]

In effect, the Fed discount window will become the 'choke point,' and thus the 'focal point,' at which our limiting bank lending solely to healthy forms of credit-extension takes place.[39] It will be, in other words, a twenty-first-century rendition of Glass-Steagall separation between productive primary, and merely speculative secondary, market investment.[40]

Before diagramming the new People's Fed pictorially, it should be noted that it is possible to 'work up' to the full arrangement via a number of routes. One is to start with what I call 'inclusive value ledgers' (IVLs) at local, state, or regional levels of fiscal and monetary governance, along the lines of this author's 'Empire State Inclusive Value Ledger' proposal now before the New York State Legislature. Another is to lever the existing system of 'Treasury Direct' accounts, through which anyone may

---

[35] Id.

[36] 'The business of banking' is a term of art in finance-regulatory parlance, connoting those features of a firm's business model that subject it to bank-regulatory jurisdiction.

[37] Again, fuller elaboration is available in Hockett, *Capital Commons*, supra note 66.

[38] Again, fuller elaboration is available in Hockett, *Capital Commons*, supra note 66.

[39] Id.

[40] Id. For more on contemporary and past Glass-Steagall-style forms of market segmentation, see, for example, Hockett, *Macroprudential Turn*, supra note 53.

transact in U.S. Treasury securities with the U.S. Treasury, into a full digital banking platform simply by instructing Treasury to issue a new Treasury Bill—a 'Treasury Dollar Bill,' or 'Treasury Dollar'—valued at one Fed dollar and made legal tender by Congress. These prospects, made urgent by the April 2020 Coronavirus pandemic and the need for quick federal relief payment disbursal that it has occasioned, are elaborated briefly below in Sect. 3.4.

3.2.1.3   Pictorial Representation

Figures 3.2 and 3.3 depict Fed and private banking operations as they now normally operate, and how they will operate under the proposed reforms, respectively. Once again arrows depict flows and 'Liabs' means financial liabilities generically considered. 'Dep' means deposit liability, and 'Debt' means debt liability—two specific species of the genus 'liability.' The '$' sign in Fig. 3.2 of course signals present-day money flows, while in Fig. 3.3 it also includes Democratic Digital Dollars. Both diagrams ignore for present purposes the flows that run between the Fed and sundry non-bank issuers of liabilities both public and private—for example, Treasury and sellers of mortgage-backed securities (MBS) pursuant to QE3.

3.2.2   A Fed Price Stabilization Fund: a.k.a. A 'Peoples' Portfolio'

As noted in Chap. 2 above, another helpful tool in maintaining price stability over the course of the Green New Deal's unfolding will be a 'People's Portfolio' or Price Stabilization Fund. This fund can readily be made part of the Fed's asset portfolio, thereby further integrating the Fed's mission with the Council's mission in a manner that fits squarely within the mandate of each institution.[41] In the alternative, it can be run by the NIC in collaboration with both Fed and Treasury.

---

[41] See again Hockett, *People's Portfolio*, supra note 61, and accompanying text.

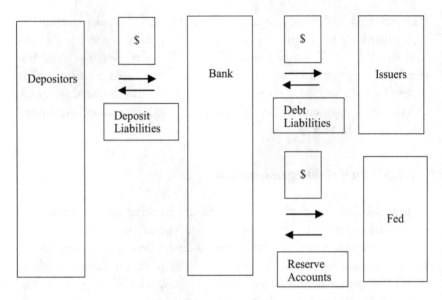

Fig. 3.2 Regular Fed/Bank arrangements and financial flows. (Source: Author's creation)

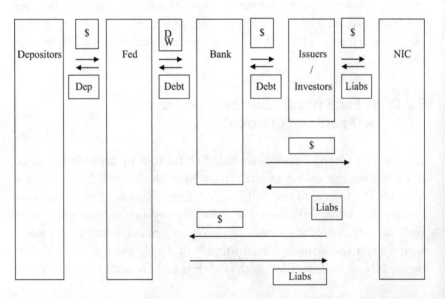

Fig. 3.3 Reformed bank/Fed/NIC relations and financial flows. (Source: Author's creation)

The idea behind the People's Portfolio is for the Fed to generalize its already well-established regime of open market operations with a view to limiting volatility in respect of more systemically significant prices than just interest rates.[42] Labor costs, commodity prices, fuel prices, and others all can be added according as seems necessary or proper in future. Indeed, any sector or subsector in which inflationary or deflationary pressures build can enjoy price modulation through Fed or NIC shorting and purchasing activity, respectively.[43]

Since the regime of Fed Taxpayer Wallets just described will bring additions to the Fed's book of liabilities, moreover, the Fed in particular will be seeking new assets in any event—to offset them. The People's

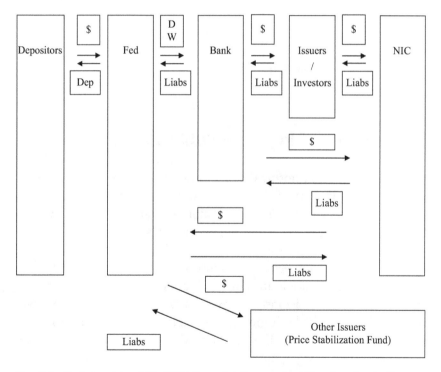

Fig. 3.4 Reformed bank/Fed/NIC financial flows w/stabilization fund. (Source: Author's creation)

---

[42] Id.

[43] See again sources cited supra, notes 61, 64, 66, and 80, and accompanying text.

Portfolio can be that book of assets, either directly or indirectly via Fed holdings of NIA issuances.[44] It will be a book that can also include, if the Fed holds it and as noted above, NIC issuances and other issuances that the Council recommends to the Fed in pursuit of its national investment mandate.[45] What we will have, then, is fully public finance that works on behalf of *all* Americans, on *both* sides—asset and liability—of the public ledger, and in primary and secondary markets alike.

Figure 3.4 supplements Fig. 3.3 by adding the Price Stabilization Fund or 'People's Portfolio.' All previously employed terms mean what they've meant in preceding diagrams. DW, added here, refers to the Fed's discount window facility—one of its principal means of lending to other institutions.[46] Again the diagram ignores for present purposes the flows that run between the Fed and sundry non-bank issuers of liabilities both public and private—for example, Treasury, sellers of mortgage-backed securities (MBS) pursuant to QE3, or sellers of other issuances pursuant to new facilities opened by the Fed in response to the spring 2020 pandemic.

3.3   State and Regional Public Banks

The new NIC and reformed Fed as just sketched operate primarily, though not solely, at the federal level. But as noted above in Chap. 2, a Green New Deal Finance Plan should aim to honor principles of federalism—or subsidiarity—as much as possible. This is necessary both as a matter of democratic justice and as a matter of effectiveness: Residents of specific localities know better than most what their needs are, including what their financial needs are. And both public and private sector entities—including financial institutions—that operate at the local level will in general tend to be both more accountable, and hence responsive, to expressions of such need. This recommends systems of state and locally

---

[44] See again sources cited supra, notes 61 and 66, and accompanying text.
[45] Id.
[46] Id.

operating public banking institutions that can work in collaboration with the NIC and reformed Fed as just sketched.

3.3.1   Regional Public Banks

At the regional level, the NIC structure as elaborated above includes Regional NIC Banks analogous to Regional Federal Reserve Banks. The idea here is to afford the Council, like the Fed, 'eyes and ears,' as well as physical facilities, 'on the ground' that are attentive and responsive to regional variations in economic condition and infrastructural need. In effect, they are meant to mediate between local institutions and enterprises on the one hand, and the two federal institutions that they operate under on the other hand. The NIC Regionals will operate as described above. The regional Fed Banks will operate as they have since 1913, with the one change being that their mandates also will reflect the changes to the Fed's mandate itself just described.

3.3.2   State Public Banks

One implication of the Fed reforms laid out above is that privately owned banking institutions will still be able to play a role in extending and allocating credit, but will only be able to do so in ways that conform to Fed discount window lending conditionality.[47] In effect, speculative bank lending for secondary and tertiary market purposes will end, with the latter form of conditionality functioning as a form of de facto restored Glass-Steagall-style categorical separation between banking functions and secondary market trading.[48] Private sector banks also will not be gen-

---

[47] The Fed lays out exacting criteria in stipulating what kinds of commercial paper and other financial instruments it stands ready to accept and thereby 'monetize' at the discount window. The discount window function can thus be analogized to the 'conforming loan' requirements that have historically been imposed by the Federal Housing Administration (FHA) and the GSEs associated with it. It will accordingly also play, under the regime proposed here, the role that Glass-Steagall used to play in the realm of financial regulation, prior to the ill-fated reforms of the Gramm-Leach-Bliley Act signed into law in late 1999. See generally Hockett, sources cited supra, notes 53, 57, 61, 66, and accompanying text.

[48] See again sources cited id.

eral deposit-takers any longer, hence will not be receiving 'other people's money' to gamble with. They will accordingly be pure investment institutions, with most if not all investments having effectively to be pre-cleared with the Fed's discount window administrators.[49]

This new arrangement also will open the door to a broader proliferation of public banks of the BND variety described above. There are two reasons. The first is that those drawn to the banking industry for whom profit motives are secondary will no longer have secondary profit-related reasons to make their careers at privately owned rather than public banks any longer.[50] Banking will indeed be 'boring again,' in a manner that renders public banking at least as interesting as private banking to aspiring bankers.[51] The second reason is that states will have heightened reason to establish public banks in order to 'capitalize on' the new investment opportunities opened both by the new NIC and by the reformed Fed as described above—not to mention the just-announced new Fed Municipal Liquidity Facility described below.

State public banks will be very well situated to liaise both between state governments and the regional Fed and NIC Banks, and between sub-state municipalities and those same regional institutions. Many states are apt to find them desirable on that account. Adding in the fact that private sector banks will be 'boring again' for the reasons just noted, and state residents drawn to banking will be much more apt to push for the establishment of such institutions than before as well.[52] The new NIC and the Fed reforms just elaborated, in short, are likely to trigger a broader 'renaissance' of public banking, and this will fill all remaining 'gaps' between federal and local finance in the name of developing a truly participatory Green New Deal across every town, village, and hamlet in the nation.[53]

---

[49] Id.
[50] See generally Robert Hockett, *Finance without Financiers*, in REAL UTOPIAS: DEMOCRATIZING FINANCE (Erik Olin Wright ed., 2020), forthcoming. For more detail, see Hockett, *Capital Commons*, supra note 66.
[51] Id.
[52] Id.
[53] Id.

3.4   Building Up from Local or from Treasury: Inclusive Value Ledgers and Complementary Currencies

It is possible that federal establishment of a National Investment Council and a reconfigured Fed along the lines just recommended will take more time than some states or localities wishing to make counterpart reforms wish to wait. It is also possible, as the Coronavirus pandemic of spring 2020 necessitates rapid Congressional appropriation and Treasury disbursal of relief payments throughout the country, that an already-existing network of universal Treasury accounts—'Treasury Direct'—will have to be made into a national payments platform immediately while development of counterpart Fed functionality takes place. Here, then, I will lay out some possible 'way-stations' en route to the Democratic Digital Dollar and People's Fed arrangements prescribed just above.

Where subnational units of government are concerned, there are of course constitutional and feasibility constraints on how much can be done along the lines here envisaged. But much nonetheless *can* be done. It can be done by exploiting both (a) the centrality of *payments* systems and associated platforms to all *monetary* systems, and (b) new technologies that render *public provision*—including subnational public provision—of such platforms a straightforward proposition.

States or cities that adopt some version of the script laid out below can accordingly speed up effectuation both of pandemic response efforts in the short term and of a Green New Deal in the medium term with their own residents even before the nation as a whole is doing so, and can *catalyze* the *nation's* doing so by proving such things feasible. We can think of such measures as subnational trial programs or 'proofs of concept' (POCs).[54] Similarly, the U.S. Treasury can develop and issue a protoversion of the Democratic Digital Dollar—a Democratic Digital 'Greenback,' as it were—even before the Fed develops a full system of individual Taxpayer Wallets.[55] The need of rapid relief payments in

---

[54] The author is working with states and cities on several such POCs now, as will shortly be noted.
[55] The familiar Federal Reserve Note of today grew out of the Treasury-issued 'Greenbacks' developed 50 years earlier. See Hockett, *Fintech's Future*, supra note 66.

response to the spring 2020 pandemic renders that prospect more compelling even than it was when the author first floated it years back.

In hopes of encouraging or at the very least facilitating such action wherever it might be seriously considered, this section maps out a plan of action that states or cities, 'compacts' of such, and/or the U.S. Treasury can commence as proto-renditions of the Democratic Digital Dollar plan sketched above, with a view to both (a) providing a banking and payments infrastructure to all and (b) catalyzing full national development along the same lines. It starts with general observations, then sketches state, local, and U.S. Treasury-administered renditions of the plan to put in place until a full-fledged People's Fed is established.

3.4.1   Moneys, Payment Platforms, and Inclusive Value Ledgers

Many people worldwide see needs for more widely accessible payment platforms and associated currencies for the accumulation, storage, and transfer of value. These are prerequisites to maximal commercial and financial inclusion and optimally efficient trade and payments alike. At subnational levels of government, this need is sometimes couched as the need for 'complementary' currencies or payment systems, or as the need for some form of 'community banking.' At the national level, it is often couched as the need to 'tap untapped markets,' 'democratize finance,' or 'bank the poor.'

The linkage of currency complementarity and payment system completion is not accidental, whether advocates realize this or not. A currency is simply what 'counts' for purposes of accounting—that is, for measuring and transferring stored value—within a payments architecture. It is a 'token' that betokens quantifiable value as accumulated, stored, and transferred within any such system. Hence it is 'that which accumulates' and 'that which pays' as productive participants in any market exchange economy earn, save, and spend 'purchasing power'—that is, spendable wealth. To supply such an architecture to any community of any size is accordingly to supply that community both with a currency and, in consequence, with a means to produce, earn, accumulate, store, measure, and transfer wealth. It is to supply that community with a monetary medium, a payments platform, a commercial infrastructure, and a rudimentary banking and financial system all in one go.[56]

New P2P digital payments technologies that have developed over the past decade now make the construction of such platforms a simple and straightforward proposition.[57] All that is needed is a digital infrastructure of 'wallets,' like the Taxpayer Wallets discussed above, that can be credited and debited through a pooled 'master account.' The latter for its part can take the form either of the public fisc of the governmental unit in question or of a legal trust settled and administered by that unit—including a special purpose vehicle (SVP) of the kind through which the Fed administers many of its lending facilities even today.[58]

Value accumulation and storage then can be done through these individual wallets or accounts, simply by enabling payment into and storage within them. Value transfer—that is, 'payment'—from any payer to any payee can for its part be effected through simultaneous crediting and debiting of payee and payer wallets.[59] 'Real-time clearing and settlement,' long a holy grail to commercial and financial market participants, thereby can be made readily available to all—literally all, without 'middlemen'— even now, if but publicly supplied as the critical market infrastructure that it in effect is in any exchange economy or commercial society such as our own.[60]

---

[56] See again Hockett, *Rousseauvian Money*, supra note 66; Hockett, *Democratic Digital Dollar*, supra note 89; and Hockett, *Payment Polyphony and Monetary Hierarchy*, working paper (2019) on the linkages noted in this paragraph; Hockett, *Digital Greenbacks*, supra note 89.

[57] See Robert Hockett, *The Capital Commons*, supra note 66, for more on the matters described in this paragraph. Also Hockett, *Democratic Digital Dollar*, supra note 89.

[58] See, for example, Hockett, sources cited supra note 90.

[59] This sequencing, whereby 'vertical' public/private monetary relations enable and optimize 'horizontal' private/private monetary relations, is fully elaborated in Hockett, *Rousseauvian Money*, supra note 66, and Hockett, *The Capital Commons*, supra note 66. It also is fully exploited in all renditions of the Digital Dollar Platform Plan developed below.

[60] It bears noting that the Federal Reserve shares this goal with sufficient urgency as to broach making it available to all. Unfortunately, it continues to envisage making it 'available to all' only by making it available to *banks*, which do not *include* all. See, for example, Federal Reserve Board of Governors 'Federal Reserve announces plan to develop a new round-the-clock real-time payment and settlement service to support faster payments,' August 5, 2019, available at https://www.federalreserve.gov/newsevents/pressreleases/other20190805a.htm

Any such system, if made available to all constituents of the governmental unit or consortium of units that furnishes it, will then amount to a universally inclusive commercial and financial architecture within that unit's jurisdiction. It will afford easy, fast, frictionless means of producing, earning, accumulating, storing, and measuring wealth, as well as means of real time transfer of such wealth with cash-reminiscent 'finality of payment' in any transaction, within the relevant jurisdiction.[61]

An added benefit of any such system comes with its enabling users to sidestep the present-day confusion of multiple private sector, for-profit middle-man payment companies, all operating with their own incommensurable protocols. Under this chaotic 'system' of private payment service providers, a multitude of platforms (a) 'interface' with one another in varyingly effective and friction-prone ways, (b) interpose barriers, complications, transaction-costs, delays and associated risks between parties and counterparties in the payments process, and (c) afford a large and still-growing number of for-profit entities with multiple socially unnecessary and costly rent-taking opportunities.[62]

Any unit of government can now easily and inexpensively supply a uniform and universally accessible such saving and spending infrastructure, thereby cutting out all of the inefficiencies and rent-taking opportunities occasioned by today's Byzantine set of arrangements. Compacts of state or local governments can do likewise. All each need do is afford every constituent with a digitally accessible wallet that 'interfaces' with its own fisc or some other universal account organized as a publicly administered entity or legal trust.

The unit of government in question then can make P2P payments (e.g., tax rebates, procurement expenditures, entitled benefits, and the like) and receive P2P payments (e.g., taxes, fees, fines, and the like) 'vertically' in real time through the medium of such accounts, simply by

---

[61] How such a system facilitates measurement, storage, and voluntary transfer of value is presumably obvious to all. How it facilitates value production is more fully laid out below. The short answer is that value—in the form of access and resources—is used in the production of value itself, while money and credit are the means of access to resources in any exchange economy such as ours. Insufficient money and credit accordingly mean insufficient access, which in turn means insufficient value-productive activity.

[62] See Hockett, *Democratic Digital Dollar*, supra note 89.

crediting or debiting them. Similarly, it can facilitate real time 'horizon-tal' P2P payments among participating constituents themselves simply by affording means of simultaneously crediting payee and debiting payer accounts in accordance with payer instructions conveyed via chip card, strip card, or smart device app.[63] And, by assuring interoperability with networks of ATMs and the like, it can ensure ready availability of older payment forms—cash—too.

Here are brief sketches of how this can be done by states, localities, compacts, and even by Treasury en route to a full People's Fed.

3.4.2   A State Inclusive Value Ledger Plan

A state payments platform and associated system of digital wallets, made interoperable with other payment forms including ATM cash, is easily constructed and administered. Practically speaking, it is probably best to proceed through two stages.

In the first stage, the state provides a digitally accessible wallet—we can call it a 'Digital Dollar Account'—to all legal residents within its jurisdiction.[64] Each such account will be P2P-linked to a pooled 'Master Account' that can be either the state fisc itself or a separate account and

---

[63] Id. These two modalities of P2P transaction—between public and private and between private and private—are the mutually complementary and indispensable 'vertical' and 'horizontal' dimensions of all monetary relations as elaborated in Hockett, *Rousseauvian Money*, supra note 66 and Hockett, *The Capital Commons*, supra note 66. They correspond to Stages 1 and 2 of the plans elaborated below.

[64] This stage corresponds to money's ineluctable 'vertical' dimension as elaborated in Hockett, *Rousseauvian Money*, supra note 66 and Hockett, *The Capital Commons*, supra note 66. The author has designed such a plan for the state of New York and drafted accompanying legislation, which has now been proposed in the state legislature by Assemblyman Ron Kim and Senator Julia Salazar. See Robert Hockett, *The New York Inclusive Value Ledger: A Peer-to-Peer Savings and Payments Platform for an All-Embracing and Dynamic State Economy*, 79 Administrative Law Review __ (2019) (forthcoming), available at https://papers.ssrn.com/sol3/papers.cfm?abstract_id=3470923. Also Robert Hockett & Ron Kim, 'New Currency for New York's Poor,' *New York Daily News*, October 28, 2019, available at https://www.nydailynews.com/opinion/ny-oped-new-currency-for-new-yorks-poor-20191029-uevs4nbx7fdwtbrlzgerdos664-story.html; and Robert Hockett & Ron Kim, 'Dynamic Inclusive Money for a Dynamic Inclusive Economy,' *The American Prospect*, October 17, 2019, available at https://prospect.org/economy/dynamic-inclusive-money-economy/. The white paper on the Plan is available here: http://ronkimnewyork.com/downloads/The-New-York-Inclusive-Value-Ledger-Sept-2019.pdf

associated SPV established as a state enterprise or legal trust. The account might be called something like the state 'Revenue Collection and Benefit Disbursement Fund,' in keeping with the fact that residents of most U.S. states pay taxes, licensing fees, fines, and the like under multiple headings, and receive rebates and benefits under literally scores of state pension, social service, and other programs.[65] The account also might be given some more attractive name—the 'Empire Fund' in New York, for example, or the 'Bear Flag Fund' in California or 'Ad Astra Fund' in Kansas.[66]

The state then will make remittances owed to its residents—for example, tax rebates, procurement payments, entitled pension or other benefit payments, and the like—by crediting their individual accounts. It will correspondingly receive payments—for example, taxes, franchise fees, fines, or the like—by debiting these same accounts. In theory these credits and debits could be denominated in any measurement unit the state and its residents found convenient. Because all U.S. state transactions occur for good reason in the national currency—the dollar—however, states that institute a platform of the kind here designed will effectively be paying and being paid digital dollars—a fact that will prove helpful in connection with 'building the Plan out' in stages below.

This first stage of state implementation of the Plan can thus be viewed as a simple digitization of contemporary state fiscal operations. This will not only render state/resident payments more reliably tractable than they are under present arrangements, but also will render the conduct of state/ resident payment flows amenable to the use of new payment media such as smart phones and other devices. Indeed, to optimize the functionality of the new digitized arrangement, the state should even develop the 'app' through which state/resident payment flows are effected, or contract out

---

[65] New Yorkers, for example, pay taxes, fees, and fines, and receive benefits under, some 100 state social service and other programs (SNAP, utilities payment assistance, pension benefits, etc.). Id.

[66] New York bills itself as 'the Empire State,' while California once was 'the Bear Flag Republic.' Kansas's state motto is 'Ad Astra Per Aspera.' It is a surprisingly pleasant exercise to think up fund names for multiple states—a 'Lone Star Fund' for Texas, a 'Quaker State Fund' for Pennsylvania, a 'Lincoln Fund' for Illinois, and so on. As a native New Orleanian, the author cannot but hope that Louisiana's fund will be named the 'Bontemps Fund.'

for design proposals.[67] In time, as multiple states implement versions of the Plan, we might even act to encourage interstate harmonization of Plans and associated apps across the U.S.

The second stage of state implementation of the Plan will be to enable payment flows not only between the state and its residents, but also among residents themselves.[68] All who hold digital P2P wallets for purposes of receiving payments from and making payments to the state will be enabled to transact with one another in 'real time' just as they transact with the state. Instead, for example, of directing that her wallet be debited as the state account is correspondingly credited, as in a tax or licensing fee remittance to the state fisc, a payer will direct that her account be debited as some *other, private* sector payee's account is correspondingly credited—just as in any private sector commercial or financial transaction.

In principle, the transition from Stage 1 to Stage 2 of Plan implementation involves no fundamental change in technical requirements or associated challenges. It is simply a matter of adding an additional layer of payment 'wiring'—an exercise that has long since become 'old hat' to fintech and crypto-currency designers. The only new task implicated by the added connectivity is the tracking of simultaneous P2P creditings and debitings of Private/Private transaction wallets in addition to the P2P creditings and debitings of Private/Public transaction wallets. That means more 'workload' in an aggregative sense, but because digital payments are overwhelmingly automated, the *practical* workload effect is *de minimis*.

It is easy to visualize the Democratic Digital Dollar Plan in operation at the state level of government as just described. That is thanks to the Plan's simplicity—a simplicity enabled by contemporary P2P payments technologies that effectively render actual payment dynamics structurally isomorphic to double-entry book-keeping, which is in turn no more

---

[67] The author has developed such an app with a colleague in the tech sector, which will be freely available. He and a number of state legislators have also been meeting with tech consultants in connection with a number of state versions of this plan now under consideration.

[68] This stage corresponds to money's 'horizontal' dimension as elaborated in Hockett, *Rousseauvian Money*, supra note 66 and Hockett, *The Capital Commons*, supra note 66. Also Hockett, sources cited supra, notes 89 and 133.

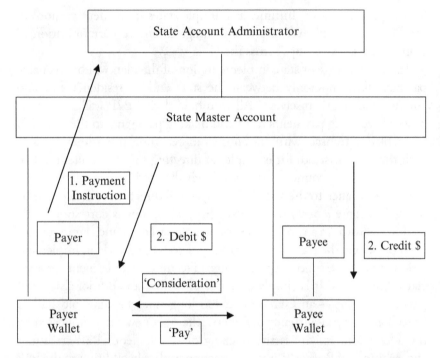

Fig. 3.5 State-administered inclusive value ledger payments system. (Source: Author's creation)

complex than the Algebra from which it derives.[69] Figure 3.5 exhibits the structure of payment flows under the Plan.

In the diagram, non-arrowed lines represent institutional linkages and arrowed lines represent payment instructions and associated flows. The payer agrees to pay the payee for some contractual consideration. Payment occurs when the payer instructs the Master Account Administrator, via a chip card, strip card, or smart device app (step 1), to debit her own wallet in the Master Account and correspondingly credit the payee's wallet in the Master Account (step 2). At Stage 1 of Plan implementation, counterparties in any such transaction will comprise one public and one private sector 'peer.' At Stage 2 of Plan implementation, all wallet holders in

---

[69] See again Hockett, sources cited id.; and Hockett *Payment Polyphony and Monetary Hierarchy*, supra note 126, on these linkages.

the system, public or private, will be able to make and receive payments to and from one another in the same manner.

It will be necessary at Stage 1, and desirable at Stage 2, to provide for commercial bank interoperability with the Plan Master Account, in order that state residents be enabled to spend out of their Digital Dollar Wallets into the broader economy, and to withdraw traditional cash if desired, when they're in surplus. This can be done either by (a) requiring that commercial banks provide connectivity, including ATM connectivity, between individual Digital Dollar Wallets and bank transaction accounts, (b) holding Master Account funds themselves in the form of Plan commercial bank transaction wallets, (c) establishing a state bank, roughly

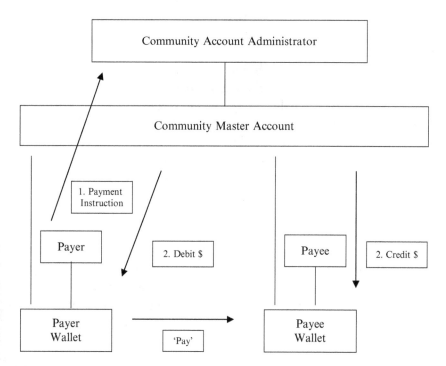

Fig. 3.6   Community-administered inclusive value ledger system. (Source: Author's creation)

along the lines of the BND model,[70] to assist in administering the Plan, or (d) any combination of these three modalities.

3.4.3   The Community ('Complementary') Value Ledger Plan

The community rendition of the Digital Dollar Plan can be thought of as a structurally identical or near-identical, but jurisdictionally and practically more limited, case of the state rendition. It is structurally identical or near-identical in that the simple P2P structure manifest in Fig. 3.5 above can be retained with no more than a few labeling changes or other additions to represent it, as Fig. 3.6 below does. It is jurisdictionally and practically more limited in that localities are creatures of state law in the American constitutional order, state-charted as municipal corporations and endowed only with such functions and authority as states affirmatively confer upon them.

Though the decision whether to permit local renditions of the Plan rests ultimately with states, there is good reason for states to permit, encourage, and facilitate their adoption and spread among localities. The principal reason is, non-accidentally, identical to that for 'community,' or 'complementary,' currencies as advocated by many proponents of greater commercial and financial inclusion—non-accidentally because, as noted above, a currency simply is 'that which counts' for purposes of accounting in any value-storage and -payments system.

One entailment of the 'money as "that which counts"' truism is that if a given quantum of potential value exceeds a given currency stock's capacity fully to express and convey that value, potential value can fail to be fully 'realized.' Potential wealth will in such case be 'left' on the proverbial 'table.' People will not produce as much as they can potentially produce in this circumstance, for the means of securing command over productive resources ('purchasing power'), and of being remunerated for productive

---

[70] See Bank of North Dakota Homepage, supra note 75.

services ('earning power'), will be lacking in precisely the same measure as the money supply is lacking.[71]

This correlation between potential value-creation and monetary value-expression is precisely why the U.S.'s first Treasury Secretary, Alexander Hamilton, made establishment of a national bank and issuance of a new monetary medium his first priority upon taking office with a view to setting the new nation on a path to productive and inclusive prosperity.[72] It is also why all modern nations maintain central banks or monetary authorities charged with issuing and administering what now are referred to in monetary parlance as 'elastic currencies.'[73]

Supplies of elastic currencies can be extended when there remains productive potential yet to be realized (i.e., when there is 'capacity-underutilization,' or 'slack'). They can, symmetrically, be modulated or contracted when they exceed what is necessary for productive use as distinguished from inflationary expenditure (i.e., expenditure upon no longer expanding supplies of goods and services sold in an economy already operating at full capacity). Modern central banking just is the art and science of modulating extensible and contractible elastic currency supplies, with a view to maintaining sustainable balance between 'money supplies' and 'productive potential.'[74]

States and localities, unfortunately, do not have authority to institute central banks or monetary authorities able to issue and manage their own elastic currencies. When there are frictions or barriers between varyingly 'isolated' communities and the broader national economy over which the nation's central bank operates, productive potential can in consequence lie fallow, with value in consequence left unproduced and untapped. This 'scarce currency' problem is familiar, of course, to many American states and especially cities and rural outposts. It is also familiar, alas, to many

---

[71] See again Hockett, *Rousseauvian Money*, supra note 66; Hockett, *The Capital Commons*, supra note 66; and Hockett, *Democratic Digital Dollar*, supra note 89; for further elaboration of these linkages.

[72] Id. Also Hockett, *Post-Liberal Finance*, supra note 35; and Robert Hockett, *A Jeffersonian Republic by Hamiltonian Means*, 79 SOUTHERN CALIFORNIA LAW REVIEW 865 (2006).

[73] Id.

[74] Id. Also Robert Hockett, *A Fixer-Upper for Finance*, supra note 57.

countries and regions in the Euro Area, which also lack domestically managed elastic currencies of their own.[75]

The idea behind 'complementary currencies' is simply to afford additional ('complementary') means—means additional to the scarce dominant currency—of expressing, capturing, and trading the value forgone in a cash-poor locality. The currency 'complemented' just is the dominant currency in which the community is 'cash-poor.'

We can thus think of supplemental currencies as 'value gap fillers,' trickling into currently inaccessible 'dry crevices' where, owing to imperfect integration with the national economy, there is presently not enough regular currency to reach. The complementary currencies in effect nourish currently undernourished 'green shoots' or 'value sprouts.' If a municipal authority can supply such a currency, it can accordingly fuel more productive activity of the kind that will ultimately not only improve life in the community, but also draw in more of the complemented currency from outside of the community as well, thereby mitigating, if not solving, the problem that necessitates complementary currencies in the first place.[76]

The institutional challenge posed by the need of a complementary currency is that municipalities lack legal authority to issue any currency that might appear to compete with the national currency. But it is easy with ordinary levying or assessing—for example, license fee-collecting, taxing, fining, and so on—authority and new P2P payments technologies, on the other hand, for a municipality to issue a rough *functional equivalent* of a traditional currency, usable within its territorial jurisdiction, that truly does *complement* and *supplement* rather than *compete* with the national currency. All that the locality needs to do is relinquish or transfer rights to the payments it is owed in a locally spendable form, while providing a local payments platform on which that local spending then can be done.

The relinquishments can be thought of as—indeed in the first instance they are likely primarily to *be*—assessment credits, just as many

[75] See Hockett, *Open the Marriage to Save It: A Complementary Digital Euro Plan* (2019), available at https://papers.ssrn.com/sol3/papers.cfm?abstract_id=3470934; and Hockett, *Money for the World: A Digital Clearing Union* (2019).

[76] See again Hockett, *Rousseauvian Money*, supra note 66; Hockett, *The Capital Commons*, supra note 66; and Hockett, *Democratic Digital Dollar*, supra note 89.

now-familiar sovereign-issued currencies appear originally to have been or betokened.[77] Various forms of locally value-adding activity then can be remunerated in these credits, which at Stage 1 of implementation can be locally permitted to be conveyed to the municipal authority in lieu of national currency in fulfillment of the payment obligations that it levies. Then at Stage 2 the locality can facilitate transfers among constituents themselves of these same instruments, such that a local resident might pay a local retailer, for example, in assessment credits ultimately payable to the municipality in discharging assessment obligations.

These latter credits can, once again, in theory be measured in any unit the local authority that establishes the payment platform, along with its electoral constituents, sees fit to establish. But as in the state case above, so here it makes sense to denominate in the national currency to facilitate both (a) ready interoperability with that currency, especially as it comes to be digitized on a national payments platform as envisaged below, and (b) associated fuller integration with the national economy. For the same reasons it will be desirable to ensure interoperability between individual Digital Dollar Wallets and more traditional banking facilities including ATMs.

Stages 1 and 2 as just described of course replicate counterpart stages in implementation of the state version of the Plan sketched above. That is no accident. Through the simple device of a master account and a system of (now local) Digital Dollar Wallets as sketched above, the locality can first P2P-transact with its own constituents much as do states in the State Digital Dollar Plan (Stage 1), then enable P2P transactions among constituents inter se, also as in the State Digital Dollar Plan (Stage 2). All that will differ in most cases will be the size of the plan in both dollar value and participant population terms, though of course large city plans will be larger than small state plans. Pictorially, then, things will look much as in Fig. 3.6.

---

[77] See again Hockett, *Rousseauvian Money*, supra note 66.

3.4.4   Inter-City, Inter-State, or Regional 'Compact' Ledgers

The smaller size of many community plans as just schematized might recommend use of a larger financial institution for purposes of administering the Plan's Master Account. This could be done, for example, by making use of a commercial bank trust department or other private sector fiduciary, with multiple municipalities banding together to bargain for optimal terms. Better still would be for municipal plans to participate in state plans, 'plugging in' to State Master Accounts, be these directly state-managed or state-delegated to commercial or public banks patterned after the Bank of North Dakota.[78]

By the same token—pun ratified if not originally intended—we can imagine states forming multi-state *regional compacts* as well with a view to facilitating broader participation in a gradually growing interstate public payments platform and associated deepening economic integration. (Ditto state members of the Eurozone, whose economic isolation within the Euro Area partly reflects the latter's not being what is known in the discipline as an 'optimal currency area.'[79]) In payments parlance, smaller 'closed loop' payment systems would steadily integrate into larger such systems, gradually edging-out and replacing the nation's existing polyglot 'open loop' system—if 'system' is even the right word for the present welter of multiple rent-extractive arrangements.[80]

'Compacting' of this sort will require no separate 'Stage 1' of its own. That Stage will already have been passed through by the participating units of government that have established P2P payment platforms for

---

[78] See again Bank of North Dakota Homepage, supra note 75.

[79] See again Hockett, *Open the Marriage to Save It: A Complementary Digital Euro Plan*, supra note 144; and Hockett, *Money for the World: A Digital Clearing Union*, supra note 144.

[80] Broadly speaking, an 'open loop' payments system is one in which intermediaries—typically but not always financial institutions—stand between transacting parties and whatever party manages the relevant payments platform or infrastructure. In a 'closed loop'—alternatively, 'peer-to-peer,' or 'P2P'—system, by contrast, only a single payment platform and system administrator stand between payers and payees. See again Hockett, *Payment Polyphony and Monetary Hierarchy*, supra note 126. See also, for example, INVESTOPEDIA, *Open Loop Card*, available at https://www.investopedia.com/terms/o/open-loop-card.asp; and Investopedia, *Closed Loop Card*, available at https://www.investopedia.com/closed-loop-card-definition-4683996

their constituents. All that will remain to be done is to join separate local or state master accounts into one intercommunity or interstate master account, then install the 'wiring' needed to enable mutual P2P crediting and debiting, including for purposes of ATM cash withdrawal, by all legal persons whose state or local governments join to form the relevant compact and associated payments platform. Thereupon state, local, or both kinds of governmental unit will continue to remit and receive P2P payments vis-à-vis one another and vis-à-vis constituents through Digital Dollar Wallets of their own in the Master Account, while their constituents will also be able to transact across state or local boundaries inter se.

3.4.5   A U.S. Treasury-Administered Inclusive Value Ledger and 'Treasury Dollar' or 'Digital Greenback' Plan

The intergovernmental 'compacting' just envisaged suggests the prospect of state and local payments platforms and associated digital currencies' being 'built out' to embrace an ever-widening circle of citizens, businesses, and other residents of the U.S., all of whom will be progressively liberated both from the depredations of rent-extracting private sector 'payment service' firms and from the anti-productive economic stagnation that imperfectly available non-digital national currency still permits notwithstanding its Fed-managed elasticity. Much as digital value-storage and payment media like Alipay and M-Pesa have enabled far greater value-expression and associated value-generation in historically 'underbanked' nations like China and Ethiopia, so will Democratic Digital Dollars enable the same in the U.S. The only difference will be that here this medium of value-storage and transfer will be publicly afforded as the essential public infrastructure that it is, just like its *predecessor* payment technologies of U.S. Mint-stamped coins, Fed-issued Dollar Bills, and Treasury-issued Greenbacks, T-Bonds, T-Notes, and T-Bills.[81] Having

---

[81] See again Hockett, *Rousseauvian Money*, supra note 66; Hockett, *Payment Polyphony and Monetary Hierarchy*, supra note 126; Hockett, *Money's Past*, supra note 66; and Hockett, *The Capital Commons*, supra note 66; Hockett, *Digital Greenbacks*, supra note 66.

publicly issued these money tokens while money has been primarily material, we shall continue to do so as money becomes primarily digital.[82]

This steady expansion of digital value-storage and transfer availability to all will be facilitated—indeed, it is all but guaranteed—by the structural simplicity of the Democratic Digital Dollar Plan, which replicates that of a simple ledger or account book maintained among friends, family members, or multiple depositors holding accounts at the same bank. As straightforward as book-keeping, account-keeping, and the algebra from which accounting derives, the digital dollar platform bids fair to proliferate widely among units of political organization on the strength of its own ease of administration and its rent- and stagnation-ending fecundity.

The likelihood of such intergovernmental payments system conglomeration through 'compacts' suggests that ultimately our 'highest' level of government itself—our federal government, with its (i.e., with *our*) plenary jurisdiction over all matters monetary and commercial within our national union—will do well to build and administer a *national* Plan that includes all state and local Plans. The fact that such a system will enable optimal development of the Green New Deal as well, along the lines discussed above, suggests not only that development along these lines is probably inevitable, but also that forward movement as quickly as possible is equally desirable. Hence the Fed-administered Democratic Digital Dollar plan proposed above. On the way there, however, it might be simpler to commence with a Treasury rendition of the Plan, particularly amid pandemic such as is now underway at the time of this writing.

It is straightforward, in light of the foregoing discussion, to envisage what at least the simplest, Treasury rendition of such a plan would look like. The Treasury rendition of the Democratic Digital Dollar Plan would, yet again, be structurally identical to the state and local renditions schematized above. All that would differ, also again, would be the scale and scope of the Plan as measured by (a) the number of participating legal persons, and (b) the number of kinds of Public/Private remittance that the new payments platform would facilitate.

---

[82] Id.

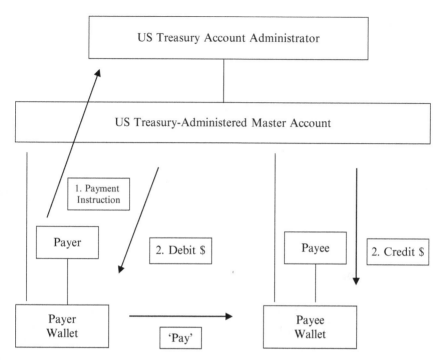

Fig. 3.7 U.S. Treasury-administered inclusive value ledger and treasury dollar system. (Source: Author's creation)

With respect to (a), all persons within U.S. jurisdiction who have occasion to transact with the federal fisc—citizens, residents, businesses—would now have P2P Digital Dollar Accounts of the kind sketched above, through which they would pay and be paid by other legal persons and governmental units with Accounts on the platform. In effect, the Master Account and Account Administrator of Figs. 3.5 and 3.6 would simply become a Treasury Master Account and the Treasury Department, respectively.

With respect to (b), the number of kinds of Public/Private remittance facilitated now would include all forms to which federal instrumentalities are party in addition to those to which state and local governmental units are party. Hence federal benefits and credits like Social Security, Federal Farm Credit loans, Small Business Administration loans and the like; procurement payments such as by the departments of Transportation,

Defense, or the like; fines and penalties; and taxes or tax refunds and credits like EITC all would now flow through the national Digital Dollar Plan pipeline.

The result would be a complete and fully integrated federal, state, and local P2P payment platform and associated Democratic Digital Dollar, with localities able to administer dollar-denominated community currency systems, states able to join and to integrate localities in that project of intrastate payment system completion, and the U.S. Treasury providing the platform through which payments flow among household, business firm, municipal, state, *and* federal 'treasuries.' As with the state and local renditions sketched above, moreover, so here implementation would proceed in two stages, beginning with the establishment of individual accounts enabling remittances between Treasury and all holders, and proceeding thence to enabling payment flows among all account holders inter se, including for purposes of ATM access to cash. Pictorially, things would accordingly look as depicted in Fig. 3.7.

All of the foregoing would be true in pretty much any period of late twentieth and early twenty-first-century U.S. history. It is probably also worth noting, however, one variant of the Treasury Plan that both could and now probably be *should* be instituted *immediately*. At the time of this writing, the U.S. Congress is authorizing direct cash payments from Treasury to U.S. citizens and businesses hard-hit by the 'social distancing' and 'shelter in place' imperatives occasioned by the spring 2020 Coronavirus pandemic. This has confronted both Congress and Treasury with an especially poignant challenge—namely, how to get payments out to the 25% of the population who are unbanked or underbanked, and how to get payments more safely and quickly—without use of paper, which is a virus vector—to the millions more who do not have 'direct deposit' arrangements with Treasury.

As it happens, Treasury already has an infrastructure ready to hand, which it could quickly expand, to handle this problem. Through Treasury Direct, anyone with a bank account and a Social Security or Taxpayer I.D. number can open a transaction account—a Treasury Direct Account, or 'TDA'—with Treasury within five minutes online, through which to transact with Treasury in Treasury securities. This means that Treasury already has, in effect, a digital infrastructure corresponding to 'Stage 1' as described above—that is, 'vertical' P2P connectivity between public fisc and individual account holders. All that is missing are two readily supplied additions—(a) 'horizontal' connectivity between Treasury Direct accounts themselves, and (b) capacity to transfer legal tender—that is, Federal Reserve Notes—between accounts.

An immediate measure that could be taken before summer of 2020, then, would be (a) for Treasury to put in place 'horizontal' connectivity between digitized TDA wallets, and (b) for Congress to authorize a new Treasury Bill—call it a 'Treasury Dollar Bill' or 'Treasury Dollar'—valued at one Federal Reserve Note per that will count as legal tender just like Federal Reserve Notes. This is the author's 'Treasury Dollar Plan' now under consideration by members of the U.S. House Financial Services Committee and the Senate Banking Committee.[83]

It is to be hoped that this plan will be adopted and implemented as quickly as possible. Then, once the spring 2020 pandemic has passed, the system can be more fully integrated with, or perhaps folded into, a full Democratic Digital Dollar and People's Fed plan such as that discussed above, as the pandemic's end allows for more painstaking fine-tuning. Summing up the foregoing, Fig. 3.7 schematizes what a Treasury Dollar Plan en route to a full Democratic Digital Dollar and People's Fed plan might look like. Terms and symbols continue to bear the same meanings they've had in prior diagrams, with the one partial exception that '$' here refers to Treasury Dollars rather than Federal Reserve Notes—a distinction that makes no difference other than in respect of issuing authority.

Again, in time this system could migrate to Fed administration and be fully integrated into the incrementally restructured Fed as sketched above. As noted earlier, this would in effect follow the script of the paper

---

[83] See, for example, Robert Hockett, *The Treasury Dollar Act of 2020*, available at https://papers.ssrn.com/sol3/papers.cfm?abstract_id=3563007; Robert Hockett, *A Treasury Dollar Plan*, available at https://papers.ssrn.com/sol3/Papers.cfm?abstract_id=3567829; Robert Hockett, 'Digital Dollars for All,' *Wall Street Journal*, April 6, 2020, available at https://www.wsj.com/articles/digital-dollars-for-all-11586215100; Robert Hockett, 'Why Now for a Treasury Dollar? Because Coronavirus,' *Forbes*, March 29, 2020, available at https://www.forbes.com/sites/rhockett/2020/03/29/why-now-for-a-digital-treasury-dollar-because-coronavirus/#1dc97a521305; Robert Hockett, 'How to Keep the Digital Dollar Democratic: A Treasury Dollar / Treasury Direct Plan,' *Forbes*, March 24, 2020, available at https://www.forbes.com/sites/rhockett/2020/03/24/how-to-keep-the-digital--dollar-democratic-a-treasury-dollar-bill%2D%2Dtreasury-direct-plan/#132acd6e37c8; Hockett, *Digital Greenbacks*, supra note 66.

dollar itself, which began as the Treasury-issued 'Greenback' in the late nineteenth century, then migrated to Fed issuance in the early twentieth century as more fine-tuned monetary operations grew in both urgency and feasibility.[84] Whether we go this route or continue to charge Treasury with this task, perhaps while working a gradual consolidation of Fed and Treasury operations as I have suggested in prior work, can be decided in future.[85]

3.5   Pictorial Summary and Synthesis

It might be helpful to summarize the financial architecture elaborated above one more time in pictorial form, now including state-level public banks and continuing (though shrunken) privately owned banks. Figure 3.5 does so. Terms, line segments, and arrows mean what they've meant in prior diagrams, with two additions: First, the horizontal arrows at bottom depict interactions with the Fed or NIC via their regional offices or subsidiaries, which can but need not be financial flows. Second, an 'issuer/investor' is a financial intermediary, which in the diagram issues to (i.e., is funded from) the left and invests (i.e., funds) to the right (Fig. 3.8).

---

[84] Id.
[85] The consolidation prospect is vetted at length in Hockett, *Capital Commons*, supra note 66.

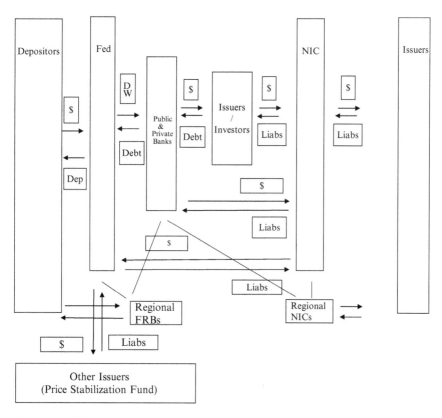

Fig. 3.8 Reformed bank/Fed/ NIC relations and financial flows. (Source: Author's creation)

4

Comparison to Lesser Alternatives

It will be helpful, before closing this monograph, briefly to describe the most oft-encountered alternatives to what is here proposed. Most such alternatives are serviceable so far as they go, but unfortunately do not go far enough. Indeed, they can be viewed as incipient or stunted renditions of particular parts of the Plan just elaborated over Chap. 3.

4.1 'Infrastructure Banks' (IBs)

One familiar family of proposals floated and, in some cases, acted upon in recent years is the cluster of 'infrastructure banks' (IBs) suggested by or encountered in various quarters. The European Investment Bank (EIB) is one familiar case in point.[1] So are, as it happens, the World Bank—whose full name is the tellingly illustrative 'International Bank for *Reconstruction* and *Development*' (emphasis added)—and the sundry regional

---

[1] The EIB was established in 1958 and is owned and operated by the EU member-states. Its mission is to foster, through a variety of public-private investment partnerships, the continued infrastructural development and economic integration of the European Union. See EIB website, available at https://www.eib.org/en/index.htm

© The Author(s) 2020
R. C. Hockett, *Financing the Green New Deal*,
https://doi.org/10.1007/978-3-030-48450-7_4

development banks that work in conjunction with it: the Inter-American Development Bank (IADB), the African Development Bank (ADB), & cet. The author of the present monograph has himself developed IB proposals in the past.[2] These institutions often do salutary work, but they are also too limited for purposes of the full Green New Deal. It will be helpful briefly to summarize their advantages and disadvantages.

4.1.1 Advantages: Simpler, Much Recent Precedent Abroad

The advantages offered by the IB model are its comparative simplicity and the wealth of experience already gleaned in connection with its now-familiar operations. IBs typically work in either or both of two ways. First, they organize consortia of public and private lenders in connection with particular projects, sometimes beginning with grants extended by governments or charitable institutions. And second, they stand ready to purchase and form diversified portfolios of locally issued development bonds, thereby facilitating risk-pooling and secondary market formation.[3] In this sense they combine the primary and secondary market functions described in connection with the NIC's Investment Committee in Chap. 3 above.

How much of each of these things any one institution does is a function of its mandate and funding sources. Some IB proposals, for example,

---

[2] See, for example, Nation Building Here at Home Act of 2012, H.R. 4352, 112th Cong. (2012), available at https://www.congress.gov/112/bills/hr4352/BILLS-112hr4352ih.pdf; and Robert Hockett, *White Paper in Support of the Nation Building Here at Home Act of 2012* (2012), available at https://papers.ssrn.com/sol3/papers.cfm?abstract_id=2029239. For previous domestic precedent, see, for example, National Infrastructure Bank Act of 2007, S. 1926, 110th Cong. (2007), available at https://www.congress.gov/110/bills/s1926/BILLS-110s1926is.pdf; National Infrastructure Bank Act of 2007, H.R. 3401, 110th Cong. (2007), available at http://www.gpo.gov/fdsys/pkg/BILLS-110hr3401ih/pdf/BILLS-110hr3401ih.pdf; National Infrastructure Development Act of 2007, H.R. 3896, 110th Cong. (2007), available at https://www.congress.gov/110/bills/hr3896/BILLS-110hr3896ih.pdf; *Fiscal Year 2016 Budget Overview*, OFFICE OF MGMT. & BUDGET, http://www.whitehouse.gov/omb/overview (last visited July 5, 2015); Joseph Weber, *Obama to Propose $50B in Infrastructure Projects*, WASH. TIMES (Sept. 6, 2010), http://www.washingtontimes.com/news/2010/sep/6/obama-propose-50b-infrastructure-projects/

[3] See, for example, HEIDI CREBO-REDIKER & DOUGLAS REDIKER, FINANCING AMERICA'S INFRASTRUCTURE: PUTTING GLOBAL CAPITAL TO WORK (2008), available at http://www.voltairenet.org/IMG/pdf/Financing_America_Infrastructure.pdf

have envisaged infrastructure-change as part of specific IB mandates.[4] A truly large scale such bank, acting in coordination with fiscal and monetary authorities, could do a great deal of good. Indeed one way of thinking about the National Investment Council described above is as a 'super-sized' infrastructure bank whose functions and internal structure are determined by the structure and far-reaching aims of the Green New Deal itself.

Needless to say, however, because there has been no public project of comparable scale and scope as the Green New Deal since the original New Deal and Second World War mobilizations of the 1930s and 1940s, the U.S.'s own Reconstruction Finance Corporation of that era makes for a much more apt model than does any existing infrastructure bank or proposal. And though it is less historically proximate owing to the last work along these lines' having been done in the early 1950s, this is simply because that era was the last in which we pursued any national project of the same degree of ambition as that of the Green New Deal.[5]

4.1.2 Disadvantages: Too Small in Size and Scope, Nothing on Inclusion or Democracy, Little Private Sector Involvement

The principle disadvantage of the IB model has in effect just been suggested. The problem is that all recent precedent is far too modest in scale, scope, and complexity to be adequate to Green New Deal planning or execution purposes. The Green New Deal is not just about 'infrastructure' in any narrow, 'roads and bridges' sense, even though it includes such. It is a full economic revitalization plan, with multiple Project Fields and work to do both at every level of government and by the public and private sectors alike.

---

[4] Something much like this is behind the 2008 Clean Energy Bank proposals of Senators Bingaman and Domenici and Representatives Inslee and Israel. See The 21st Century Energy Technology Deployment Act, S. 3233, available at https://www.govtrack.us/congress/bills/110/s3233; and H.R. 2212, available at https://www.govtrack.us/congress/bills/111/hr2212; and the Clean Energy Investment Bank Act, S. 2730, available at https://www.govtrack.us/congress/bills/110/s2730/text

[5] See again sources cited supra, note 80, and accompanying text.

In view of the systemic nature of the transformation the Green New Deal will effect, moreover, it must combine functions like those of the NIC elaborated above in Chap. 3 with complementary Fed and Price Stabilization Fund reforms of the kind also elaborated above in Chap. 3. In this light it is far preferable, when thinking of models and precedents, to look to the RFC of the 1930s and 1940s than to any contemporary IB.

4.2   Public-Private Partnerships (PPPs, P3s)

So-called public-private partnerships—or P3s—are not, strictly speaking, alternatives to IBs. They amount, rather, to a subspecies of IB—one that explicitly weds public with private sector institutions in pursuit of development goals. Like the IB model itself, moreover, it can take various forms and operate in various ways. Its advantages and disadvantages accordingly constitute particular variations on the disadvantages and advantages of IBs more generally.

4.2.1   Advantages: Those of IBs, Plus Credit Modulation Through More Productive Allocation of Private Investment

The advantages of the P3 model are those of the generic IB model, with one added benefit: it explicitly brings private sector institutions into the planning and execution of infrastructure projects. This in principle can yield informational ('price discovery') benefits, participation, and 'buy in,' not to mention the credit modulation and allocation advantages discussed in connection with the NIC in Chap. 3 above. In this sense, the P3 model can be understood, like the generic IB model itself, as an incipient form of the NIC designed above. It is, in a sense, the 'seed' of the fuller model.

4.2.2   Disadvantages: Those of IBs, Plus 'Capture,' Cronyism, and Other Forms of Corruption

Like its advantages, the P3 model's disadvantages *also* are counterparts to those of the limited IB model itself. In its familiar contemporary forms, it is simply too small and narrow in mandate to be suitable for purposes of the far more ambitious and systemically transformative Green New Deal.

Its small scale also renders the P3 model vulnerable to a unique danger—that of 'capture' by vested economic interests once they are let in on the act. This danger is especially pronounced in the case of the P3 model that is most often encountered—namely, that which is privately managed, with 'the public' involved only in the form of money investment. Putting public money at the unfettered disposal of private sector entities has never been a good idea. There is no reason to think it a good idea now. The Green New Deal is meant to benefit literally everyone, but it is not meant to be an additional avenue by which the financial services industry can commandeer and 'skim from the top' of a democratically conducted national transformation in the realm of planet-saving and justice-restoring productive activity.

In contrast to the typical P3 arrangement, the sheer size, scope, and jurisdictional status of the NIC's operations as described above helps to *immunize* it from 'capture' dangers. With multiple distinct Project Fields, an explicit inclusion and justice mandate, and status as an organ of the federal government, there is no single coherent private sector interest apt to be able to gain control of it.[6] This is not to say there is no danger at all of corrupting influences or improper use of office—these vulnerabilities threaten any public, just as they routinely afflict many private, institutions. It is only to say that the NIC model, in sharp contrast to the P3

---

[6] This observation mirrors, incidentally, James Madison's argument in *Federalist 10* that a continent-spanning republic is indeed sustainable owing to no single sectional interest's capacity in such case to gain the upper hand against the plethora of other interests bound to emerge in a large and far-flung polity. See Federalist, Number 10 (Madison) (1787), available at https://billofrightsinstitute. org/founding-documents/primary-source-documents/the-federalist-papers/federalist-papers-no-10/. Here is another sense in which the Green New Deal, which is as big and inclusive as America itself, is actually more feasible than are lesser, more 'humble' and 'incremental,' alternatives.

model, introduces no new dangers, and indeed helps to counteract old and familiar ones.

4.3   Social Impact Bonds (SIBs)

A final now oft-encountered proposal floated in connection with infrastructure development can be thought of as an attenuated, less formal rendition of the P3, and hence of the IB as well. The social impact bonds, or SIBs, that have drawn attention of late are financial instruments developed by private sector investment banks in collaboration with public sector entities including agencies and local governments.

The idea is to select project areas in need of public investment, develop success metrics and means of compensating investors when projects succeed as measured by those metrics, and then float bonds to investors to raise capital for the projects in question. In effect, these bonds are smaller-scale renditions of the NIC issuances described above in Sect. 3.1. This is the source of their advantages, while their 'smaller scale' is, as in the case of P3s and IBs more generally, the source of their disadvantages.

4.3.1   Advantages: Those of IBs and P3s, but Moreso

The advantages of SIBs are in essence intensifications of the advantages of P3s and IBs. Attracting private capital to public projects helps to dampen any inflationary impact that might otherwise emerge in connection with public expenditure. It also attracts 'buy-in' and associated political support from investors. And it can lever the Hayekian informational advantages that 'price discovery' in capital markets can sometimes afford through the 'noise' that otherwise afflicts those markets.[7] All of these advantages have already been elaborated in connection with NIC issuances as described above in Chap. 3.

---

[7] See again supra, note 78, and accompanying text.

4.3.2 Disadvantages: Those of IBs and P3s, but Moreso

The problem with SIBs, as for P3s and IBs more generally, stems from their piecemeal and small-scale nature, as well as the particular form of private sector involvement that they entail. SIBs are not at present conceived as parts of larger wholes—let alone of large, complex wholes like the Green New Deal—where project planning is concerned. Relying entirely on private finance as they do, moreover, they can be utilized only in connection with projects that generate immediately capturable, taxable, and transferable wealth.[8] And the role they confer upon private investment banks, as in the case of P3s, all but invites 'capture' and misuse of public resources.

The simplest way to avoid these problems is to combine all SIB issuances in one comprehensive project and associated portfolio or ensemble of portfolios, all of them guided and managed by public authority in consultation with private sector entities—entities that also include labor and productive industry rather than only Wall Street. But this is precisely what the NIC and its issuances, in collaboration with a reformed Fed, do as described above in Chap. 3. Again, then, as with P3s and IBs more generally, the best way to think about SIBs is as incipient forms of NIC issuance—forms that are not optimized until 'scaled up' in the way that the architecture mapped in Chap. 3 does.

4.4 A 'Green Reinvestment Act,' a 'Loan Guarantee & Securitization Plan,' and Other Tax and Regulatory Incentives

A final lesser alternative we might imagine might be described as a private sector banking counterpart to the social impact bond, or as a green counterpart either to the Community Reinvestment Act, to other regulatory

---

[8] See again sources cited supra, note 80, and accompanying text.

regimes, or to the U.S.'s mortgage and higher education finance programs of the twentieth century.

The latter first gave us the Federal Housing Agency and Fannie Mae in the 1930s, working to lower credit costs to home buyers by (a) federally guaranteeing mortgage loans that met certain conditions, and (b) making a secondary market in such loans so as to lessen the bank liquidity consequences of extending such loans.[9] It then gave us the Federal Guaranteed Student Loan Program and Sallie Mae, which did for higher education lending what the earlier programs, on which they were deliberately modeled, did for mortgage finance.[10]

The Community Reinvestment Act, for its part, is a late twentieth-century law enacted in the U.S. to encourage greater responsiveness to local credit and other banking service needs by participants in an industry that, during the later twentieth and early twenty-first centuries, underwent considerable consolidation.[11] In essence, banks wishing to expand either through mergers or through acquisitions were required to prove to the Fed's satisfaction, in the form of 'scores' awarded to them by the FDIC, that they were sufficiently attentive to local needs as to merit allowance to grow larger and more geographically extensive.[12]

Both the mortgage and higher education finance programs on the one hand and the CRA on the other hand were in effect federal credit allocation systems, operating much as do certain portions of the U.S. Internal Revenue Code to encourage private lenders to channel credit in particular publicly favored directions. It is easy to imagine any number of policies that could be developed to add green investment to the list of such publicly favored options. We might, for example, tax-favor 'green borrowing' as we now do corporate borrowing, or we might weight green investments held in bank portfolios at less than 100% for risk-weighted capital-regulatory purposes, as we now do with home loans and

---

[9] See again Hockett, *A Jeffersonian Republic by Hamiltonian Means*, supra note 141.
[10] Id.
[11] See 12 U.S.C. § 2901 *et seq.*
[12] Id.

government agency bonds.[13] Herein lie both the advantages and disadvantages of any such policy or set of policies.

4.4.1 Advantage: Easy Replication of Existing Programs

The advantage of this approach, of course, is the ease with which it could be done. New 'Green Credit' programs could simply replicate our mortgage and higher education finance programs, the CRA, the relevant provisions of our tax code and capital-regulatory regime, or any combination of these things. Indeed, it would be yet easier were we to adopt the Fed reforms advocated above, as the conditions attaching to Fed Discount Window lending could simply be written to include such private sector incentives or disincentives.

This ease, in turn, issues in greater *political* ease too, inasmuch as changes can accordingly be plausibly advocated as mere incrementalist, analogical extensions of strategies that are already familiar. Hence it is probably worth making moves of this sort at the front end of the Green New Deal planning and implementation process. It is a way of beginning to make headway even as we elaborate and then finalize plans for far greater leaps as prescribed above in Chap. 3.

4.4.2 Disadvantage: Just Not Enough

The disadvantage of this strategy is the mirror image of its advantage. This is that it is simply not sufficient to change patterns of finance to the degree requisite for achievement of the Green New Deal's urgency and transformative ambition. As noted above, decentralized private investment will be a part of the Green New Deal just as it has been of every great national project, including the New Deal and Second World War efforts.

But also as in the cases of those efforts, a massive degree of mobilization and coordination will be necessary if realization of the Green New

---

[13] See 12 U.S.C. § 1831 *et seq.*

Deal is to proceed both coherently and efficiently, as well as justly. Simply adapting existing incentive-tweaking programs to green purposes, then, will be helpful but not enough. Any such strategy must accordingly be considered a supplement to, not a substitute for, what is laid out above.

4.5   Supplemented Pictorial Summary and Synthesis

We can map the three lesser alternatives on most of the diagrams above in the following manner. Figure 3.1 will suffice for present purposes. First, then, remove the NIC and the regional NICs, and for most proposals the Fed and Treasury as well, while also shrinking the mandate to cover only garden variety infrastructure projects on a budget quantified in millions or billions, not trillions of dollars; the upshot will be a typical infrastructure bank proposal.

Next, along with the previous strip-down, remove the National Investment Council and replace it with a privately owned entity that invests both publicly and privately supplied money; the upshot will be a typical P3 arrangement. Finally, third, remove the public money from the second change, and limit issuers to public authorities selling project bonds through private underwriters; the upshot is a typical social impact bond issuance.

Conclusion

Much ground has been covered here. After Chap. 1's summary of the Green New Deal vision itself, Chap. 2 aimed to map all considerations in light of which a Green New Deal Finance Plan should be crafted. Chapter 3 mapped such an architecture with a view to the twin aims of (a) meeting all desiderata elaborated in Chap. 2, and (b) doing so with the least possible change to existing arrangements that is still consistent with Chap. 2's goals. And Chap. 4 briefly rehearsed all alternatives now on offer, showing how all of them are best viewed as embryonic renditions of what Chap. 3 itself proposes—renditions that must be scaled up to full Chap. 3 dimensions if they are to be suitable for a vast undertaking such as the Green New Deal.

As for next steps, there appear to be three. First, the architecture laid out in Chap. 3 should be vetted, discussed, and improved in keeping with what emerges from careful discussion. Second, statutory drafting should commence, so that there will be actual legislation to debate and further refine between now and January of 2021, when a new Congress and new President take office. And then third, the full Plan, the moment that legislation is passed, should be rolled out and put into effect with all

© The Author(s) 2020
R. C. Hockett, *Financing the Green New Deal*,
https://doi.org/10.1007/978-3-030-48450-7

deliberate speed. There will be literally only a decade to act, and literally not a moment to waste.

It might be well to close on a hopeful note. The Plan sketched above is far-reaching and complex, to be sure. But it isn't unprecedented and is by no means 'too much' or unfeasible. We have done this before. The New Deal and Second World War efforts were at least as 'big,' complex, and far-reaching as the Green New Deal will be. They too involved urgent, 'existential' threats that had to be confronted both seriously and expeditiously. And even the Dodd-Frank financial reforms enacted in 2010 were more complex and sprawling than the simple reforms and additions laid out in Chap. 3. (They were simply inadequate reforms.)

We should not, then, let scale, scope, or ambition deter us. Scale and scope are, to the contrary, precisely what is wanted at this critical moment. And ambition, accompanied by determination, will propel us forward.

Index[1]

---

[1] Note: Page numbers followed by 'n' refer to notes.

© The Author(s) 2020
R. C. Hockett, *Financing the Green New Deal*,
https://doi.org/10.1007/978-3-030-48450-7

CPSIA information can be obtained
at www.ICGtesting.com
Printed in the USA
LVHW040818280920
667265LV00004B/301